A New Look
at the
Old Commandments

George M. Ricker

EAKIN PRESS ⚡ Fort Worth, Texas
www.EakinPress.com

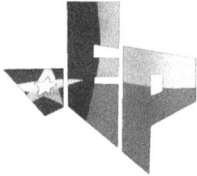

Copyright © 2005
By George M. Ricker
Published By Eakin Press
An Imprint of Wild Horse Media Group
P.O. Box 331779
Fort Worth, Texas 76163
1-817-344-7036
www.EakinPress.com
ALL RIGHTS RESERVED
1 2 3 4 5 6 7 8 9
ISBN-10: 1-68179-004-1
ISBN-13: 978-1-68179-004-8

To Frances—
Partner, companion, and confidant
in whom love reigns over law
to enrich my life
and those of our children

Contents

Foreword

The Ten Commandments are so familiar that it is difficult to imagine how a book about them could be both illuminating and traditional, in the best sense. But George Ricker manages to throw new light on this ancient subject while at the same time not straying so far afield from a mainstream understanding as to make us feel alienated. As a consequence, while Ricker takes us on a journey through perhaps unfamiliar historical material, each chapter leads us inward to a familiar center. Ricker's gentle but rigorous approach provides a model for dealing with any number of subjects hallowed by tradition but largely unexamined because assumed to be understood.

The discussion of the seventh commandment (against adultery), for example, begins with the historical point that adultery was defined as occurring only between a man (whether married or not) with a married woman. Historically, adultery was more of a property issue than one of sexual morality. But after Ricker places this commandment within its historical context, he lifts the discussion up a level into the light of an appreciation of covenant itself and how it keeps us rightly related. "Life is movement from separation to reunion and from reunion to separation," he says; and in that context, commitment keeps us loyal to our relationships in the midst of the inevitable separations and reunions of life. In his subtle, gentle way, Ricker has led us from a "you will not" into a celebration of the blessings provided by covenant, another gift of a loving God. In this, Ricker is deeply Christian, proclaiming the good news and a new commandment as emerging from the old, and thus helping us understand what it means to "fulfill the law."

How much better off we would be if all such difficult subjects were blessed with so sensitive and appreciative a guide. Perhaps then we could find common ground between the literalists of the word and the contextualists of historical understanding.

BETTY SUE FLOWERS, PH.D.
Director of Lyndon Baines
Johnson Library and Museum

Preface

We live in a permissive society. The old moral codes are not taken seriously by a majority of our population or even by some of the most conservative Christians. Few try to live by them. We do not like laws. We want the freedom to do "our thing." Anything seems to go if it serves the purpose of narrow self interest and sensual appetite.

Why, then, are we so dissatisfied? Why do we long for discipline and some authority beyond ourselves? What is behind the strong appeal of the authoritarian and conservative movements in politics and religion? Why do we hanker for a return to a less permissive age? But we cannot go back. We have been set free from the moral absolutes that were not always so moral nor absolute. Though many give lip service to a legal code, few give life service. Consciously or unconsciously we have discovered how impossible a religion of law is. No one lives by the Ten Commandments or any other law. Trying to leads us either to despair, considering how far short we come, or to pride, comparing how much better we do than some others. Most of us have found a measure of freedom from the law which, though filled with dangers, is still exhilarating.

Perhaps we are ready not for a return to the past but for another step into the future. The way forward must take seriously the contributions of the past or else we are a cut-flower people. At the same time, we cannot ignore the freedom that we have experienced in our present life. Can we not combine the two in an ethic dominated by a sense of presence?

As part of the process, I propose to take a new look at the Ten Commandments not from the perspective of absolute laws imposed upon us but as historically relative responses emerging from a loving presence experienced. If we, in some way, are sensitive to that presence, the responses we make could well be in harmony with the Decalogue that still stands as a monument to the highest and best relationship between creature and Creator and between the creatures themselves.

I offer my struggles to those of you disssatisfied with an imposed law on one side and no law on the other. I invite you to join me in a new look at the old commandments.

—George M. Ricker

Acknowledgments

As noted in the bibliography, I am indebted to many writers who have contributed to my insights. Also, I am thankful for my friend and duplicate bridge partner, Julian Martin, who read an early copy of the manuscript and made a number of helpful suggestions. In addition, I am grateful to two scholars, Dr. Leroy Howe and Dr. Stephen Reid, who read the galleys and offered appreciative words for the book cover and leaflet. My special appreciation goes to Dr. Betty Sue Flowers, Director of the LBJ Library and Museum, who wrote the Foreword. My publisher, Virginia Messer, of PenPoint Press (a division of Eakin Press) was especially helpful with the cover and overseeing the publication, and her staff was most professional with the manuscript preparation and cover/publicity material.

GMR

Introduction

Before we consider the Ten Commandments seriatim, a number of preliminary matters deserve some attention. I must begin by sharing a personal word. Some years ago I was asked, "Why don't you preach a series of sermons on the Ten Commandments?" Up to that time I had carefully avoided the subject fearful that some would assume such consideration to be a return to legalism. Thanks to the questioner, I by-passed my reluctance. The study and writing and the series of sermons that followed brought me unexpected excitement. I made surprising discoveries that helped me personally; and, consequently, I became fascinated with the new insights that emerged each week.

The Readers' First Task

At this point, I urge you, the reader, to examine Exodus 20 and Deuteronomy 5 where we find the Ten. Use a Bible or a copy of the two passages in Appendix A. Read each version and note the differences between them. Now is the time to determine your initial reaction. What do you think about the Commandments? To help you in the process, turn to Appendix B and note the Opinion Scale. If you are with a group studying the Ten Commandments, duplicate the scale and use it during the first session. Follow the instructions. Wherever you are at this point in your personal history is all right. Following this exercise in self or group disclosure, you are ready to continue.

The Origin of the Ten

Tradition tells us that God gave the Commandments to Moses. For those who take the Bible literally, the how is simple. Moses went up Mt. Sinai and God spoke to him, and after speaking God wrote the Commandments on two tablets of stone. Cecil B. DeMille's film, *The Ten Commandments*, may well have etched the how on many minds. Others prefer to see the story as a highly symbolic pointing to the long-held conviction that the Commandments came from God via Moses. Primitive memory of a mountain god and love for the Law (Psalm 119) were embedded in Hebrew minds. This memory, coupled with the inspired and creative artistry of a theologian from the southern kingdom of Judah, has given us this amazing story.

The Torah (the first five books of Hebrew Scripture) included the Ten Commandments. For centuries most of the material was part of an oral tradition. Although archaeological evidence tells us that an alphabet was developed in the Sinai and some parts of the Torah written, the greatest part of the five books was first transcribed between 1000 and 900 BCE. At least three revisions followed with later sections added, according to most Hebrew scholars.

The moral code of the Hebrews, formed in the Sinai, was not without precedent. Prior to Moses, Abraham and his family left Ur of Chaldees (Babylonia) to migrate around the fertile crescent. What they left was a land known for its ethical sensitivity. We see in the Babylonian Code of Hammurabi, dating back to about 2,000 BCE, an elaborate code of laws to insure justice. Parallels to this Code can be found in the Hebrew Torah or Law.

However we regard the process, by fiat or development, the primary figure is Moses. As Abraham is regarded as the father of the Hebrew nation, Moses is the father of Hebrew religion. He was a combination of priest, prophet and statesman. The secret of his spirit is lost in antiquity. We analyze the Scriptures only to discover that an inexplicable element marks his genius. Whatever we say about him, a residuum defies explanation. In some way Moses was a channel for the Ten Commandments and we are indebted to him and his God consciousness for the simplicity and objectivity of the Ten.

How the Hebrew people under Moses emerged from the wilderness of Sinai with the Ten, and other portions of the Torah, is a mystery. The Sinai Peninsula had practically no cities, an almost barren terrain, no remnants of kingdoms, little water, and hardly any vegetation. This is part of the wonder of the Exodus event.

Sir William Flinders Petrie, an English archaeologist, made a Sinai discovery in 1905. He found a script resembling Hebrew letters dating back to 1800 BCE. Petrie marveled at the ancient Hebrew concept of a god who demanded a code of morality for everyone. As Leonard Shlain has expressed it: "The codes of Draco, Solon, and Justinian, the Magna Carta, the U.S. Constitution, and the Miranda rights can all be traced back to what happened in the Sinai."[1]

Shlain opines that it is no coincidence that the first book written in an alphabet is the Hebrew Torah. He suggests that the Hebrew miracle was not the Red Sea nor the deliverance from slavery, but the reduction of Egyptian hieroglyphics and Sumerian cuneiform from thousands to two dozen symbols forming the first alphabet.[2] (He may be wrong about that since a thirty-character cuneiform alphabet dating back to this same period was found in Syria in about 1929.)

Yet, the mystery remains. How the Ten and a radically different concept of God emerged from "the middle of a desert, to a group of escaped slaves teetering on the edge of survival far from the centers of learning, is one of the great puzzles of all time."[3]

The Commandments have an amazing history. As part of

the Torah (Law) they constituted the primary entity that formed community. During the conquest of Canaan, the development of the monarchy, and the later collapse of both the northern and southern kingdoms, the Law (with the Ten Commandments as the core) became the framework for a people who agreed to live in community. Whatever the outward circumstances, the Law remained as the pillar.

Today the Ten Commandments, as a document, has induced much public controversy. The displaying of the Ten in public places has polarized many in our country. This book is not intended to address that controversy. My best word on the subject is simply the assertion that freedom of religion must, from my perspective, include freedom from religion for those of our citizenry who do not want themselves or their children exposed to religious symbols or material. This applies also to adherents of religions that do not have the Ten Commandments and oppose their being displayed in public places.

Another issue, missed by advocates for the public display of the Ten, is the fact that the ancient Hebrew writing had no numbered verses. This means that the Ten Commandments are variously designated by different religious groups. Some churches separate the often numbered Second into two parts. Others divide the Tenth. This means that any display of the Ten represents a public acknowledgment of some religious tradition. Jews have a different ordering than Christians. Roman Catholics and Lutherans have one numbering system while Anglicans, Eastern Orthodox, Presbyterians, United Methodists, and Baptists have another.

Of special interest is the fact that the Hebrew word translated "commandment" in English (Exodus 34:28) is more accurately translated as "word" or "saying," with several other possibilities according to Hebrew scholars. We were given the word "commandment" thanks to the King James Bible and its English predecessors. *The New English Bible* translates the passage as "Ten Words" with a footnote: "Ten Commandments." *The Revised Standard and New Revised Standard Bibles* translate the same passage as "Ten Commandments" with a footnote: "Ten Words."

The Nature of the Commandments

The Ten are often called the Decalogue or The Moral Code. Their very existence implies a moral order in creation. The Commandments serve as a restraining force to counter human temptation to both idolatry and injustice. They represent an ideal—a vision of the right relationship between creature and Creator and between the creatures themselves. They have persisted down through the centuries in spite of efforts to create something better. A teacher of an ethics class assigned his students the task of creating a new set of commandments to be relevant for today. The class then tried to form a composite from the best offering of class members. When they compared the result with the Ten Commandments, the unanimous opinion was that the original Ten were superior in simplicity and objectivity.

Ethics Today

Two views on ethics stand today in stark contrast. One is heteronomous—ethical standards in the form of norms imposed on us from the outside. The outside can be the Bible, the Church, the mores of the community or the laws of the society. The other is autonomous—standards coming from the inside which are self-motivated. The latter is best expressed by allowing each one to do his/her own thing as long as the rights of others are not ignored.

Children need ethical structures imposed from the outside. Every parent has required a child to do or not to do something. And there is a child in each of us that often needs the word from outside. The judgment about right and wrong from some respected authority can be of great help at times. However, if we adults allow our ethics to be completely determined by standards from outside, we are at best, children, or at worst, slaves.

On the other hand, ethics emerging from the inside can result in another form of slavery—to our own whims and fancies. The human creature is quite adept at justifying almost any behavior that serves self interest. Lorenzo Sadun, a professor of mathematics at the University of Texas at Austin, writing for the *Austin American-Statesman* has this insightful word:

> "In the Jewish tradition, there is a distinction between a good deed that is commanded (a mitzvah) and a spontaneous act of goodness. All else being equal, the first is considered more meritorious than the second. The rabbis explained that a spontaneous act might or might not be repeated. Fulfilling a commandment, however, is an act of humility and an acceptance or responsibility. This acceptance naturally leads to additional good deeds in the future."

Sadun's word challenges our thinking, but must we choose between the outside or the inside or is there an alternative? Are we bound either to follow some outside authority or to tune into our own inner needs and wants? I am convinced that a third alternative is available that involves responding to what is going on between or among us. We can call this a theonomous ethic directed by the One who meets us in community. In his life and teachings, Jesus of Nazareth took seriously, but not absolutely, the Hebrew law (Torah). The Gospel writers present Jesus as fulfilling the law by building on and not being buried in it. He was aware of a Presence that leads us out of dependence on either the outside or the inside. We submit not to a law or to ourselves but to a Presence that is always between and among us.

Grace is prior to law. The Hebrews knew that. In their ordering of the Ten Commandments, the first is: "I am the Lord your God, who brought you out of the land of Egypt, out of the house of slavery." (Ex. 20:2) How strange! We don't see that as a commandment. All Christian listings begin the series with the next verse. What we have failed to note is the implied word, "Remember!" Remember from whence you have come. Remember what happened to you. Remember your forebears. Remember how you got here. Remember your prior state. Remember! Remember! And that is the word for us. The Hebrew story is our story. Our coming to be is part of the mystery of God. How we have arrived at this moment, considering all the events and decisions that might have made it different, is another wonder. In the words of the familiar hymn: " And are we yet alive, And see each other's face? Glory and thanks to Jesus give, for his almighty grace."

Gratitude is the basis for ethics. And how do we express gratitude? By responding to that activity that is going on between and among us. So the Commandments follow the recognition of the grace of God. The Ten are simply the guidelines to what gratitude means in relationship to God and neighbor. They are like the railings on a stairway which are there for those needed moments. Again and again the Commandments are helpful in giving us a timeless perspective on the pressure points of life: money, power, ambition, sex, politics, justice, work, leisure and the elderly.

With this introductory word we are now ready to examine each of the Commandments to see whether the old Commandments are worth a new look.

QUESTIONS FOR DISCUSSION

1. How do you think the Ten Commandments came into being?
2. What does God-given mean to you?
3. If the Ten Commandments are a standard for gratitude ethics, for what were the Hebrews grateful? Why should we be?
4. What is the difference between laws that are to be obeyed and laws that are to be used as needed?
5. What are the strengths and weaknesses of ethical standards imposed from the outside? Or those emerging from inside?
6. Why is an ethic arising out of community better than the two options mentioned in 5?
7. Why does community imply the presence of a reality among us?

Notes

1. Shlain, *The Alphabet Versus the Goddess*, pg. 71
2. *Ibid*, pg. 78.
3. *Ibid*, pg. 71.

I

The One and Only

You will have no other gods before me.

As we begin our study of each of the commandments, we must not forget the basic biblical understanding: God is first known as Savior and secondarily as Law-Giver. Grace is prior to law. In the Introduction we observed that the Hebrews designated as the first commandment: "I am the Lord your God who brought you out of the land of Egypt, out of the house of slavery." For both Roman Catholics and Protestants this verse forms the introduction or background to the Ten. First is God's activity and then our response. This understanding saves us from a stark and burdensome legalism. Nowhere is this more clear than in the first of the commandments.

No Others?

"You will have no other gods before me." What do we do with this? Will we make a decision to have the one God and not gods? Is this a mere act of the will? Nonsense! No one decides that he[1] is going to have the one God or many. Each one lives bearing witness in the living of life whether she is possessed by the One or divided among the many. Yet, if a person is aware that life with its wondrous benefits comes from one source and not many, how could that person do other than give honor to the One? The Hebrew, so aware, gave affirmation to the One. There would be, therefore, no preference for others, no honoring of anything more than the one eternal reality. ("No other gods before me" can also mean over or above me.)

The gods are many, now as well as then. Because other cultures gave personal names to the gods, we are often blinded to the gods of our day who are not so named. Rome, for instance, had Apollo, Mars, Bacchus, Minerva, Venus, and Vesta—to name a few. They stood respectively for youth, war, pleasure, wisdom, love and the home. The Greeks had their counterparts. We are monotheists, we say. We have just one God. Or do we?

Our god or gods are what we trust in to give life meaning, what we rely upon for the motivation and orientation of our lives. Our gods are what we cannot do without; and the gods of our day are many. What do we live for? What do we cling to desperately? The tragedy of our day is that we tend to be professing monotheists but practicing polytheists. We are possessed by the many. Consider the truth of that statement.

Pleasure is one of the gods of our day. We live for pleasure. In the midst of the duties and responsibilities of life, we wait anxiously for the pleasurable moments. Our waking hours are often preoccupied with plans for the next fun time. Our *property* can be the idol or god as we devote our lives to acquiring the material benefits of our society. Note how often we try to keep people happy by supplying new goods to buoy sagging spirits. *Power* can be a meaning-giving center or god as we work to be in control of the world around us and the people related to us. Success in our time means climbing up the pyramid until we get to the top or close to it. *Prestige*, being well thought of by others, can be the all-consuming passion of life so that decisions are made with this center of reference. *Family* is the god for many, and everything else tends to fade out of focus in the commitment to the welfare of the family. Some *person* easily becomes the one we cannot do without; and we hold on possessively to an individual as the god or meaning-giver of our lives. *Work* is the god for many. We identify with our vocation and give an inordinate amount of time to our work. We lose our selfhood in the role we play in society. *Self* is a god as our life's pursuit is to find, preserve, protect, defend, love, cherish, and obey the almighty Me. From this perspective, religion is simply self-gratification. *Health* can become the idol if we are forever preoccupied with our physical well-being. Or some *hobby* can become an obsession until we are living for the time spent in the hobby. Many more centers could be mentioned. Make your additions to this list.

What is wrong with all these? Is not each one a good aspect of life? Of course! They are all good but not God. They are relative "goods" and not absolute. When we allow one or more to become absolute, we are in trouble. With more than one absolute, we experience the strife of the gods. Look at the following diagram. The large circle is the self and the small sphere is the center, metaphorically speaking. The x's are various aspects of our lives at varying distances from the center. Through a lifetime the distances from the center will vary. If the center is a vacuum or void, the self is open game. Several of the "goods" will try to occupy that space, each trying to become the orienting factor of life. The struggle to become the center leads to conflict. In some cases this may be between family and work or between pleasure and success. Many live today in the state of perpetual conflict.

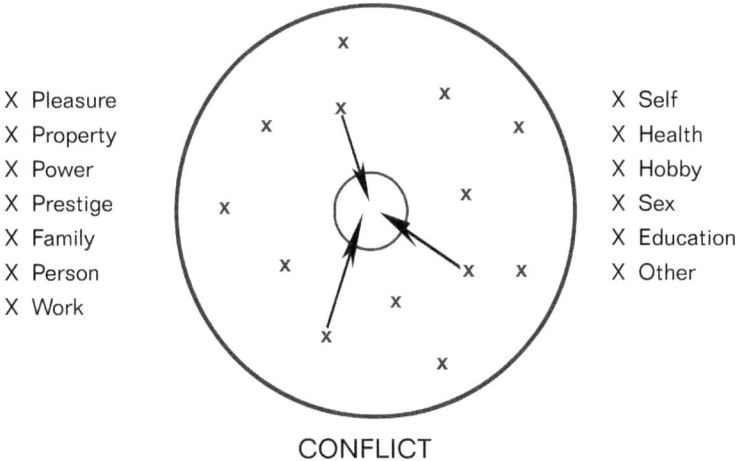

X Pleasure
X Property
X Power
X Prestige
X Family
X Person
X Work

X Self
X Health
X Hobby
X Sex
X Education
X Other

CONFLICT

None of these "goods" is absolute. Each is meaningful for a time but not always. All these "goods" are limited in ability to give satisfaction or to serve as the center of life. A few moments reflection will reveal that this is so. Take the above "gods" in order.

Pleasure is fleeting. We may cry, "Tarry a moment for you are so fair."[2] But pleasure does not tarry. Hedonists, the pleasure seekers, are always looking for the next pleasurable experience. The demand is insatiable.

Material possessions do not ultimately satisfy. "... where moth and rust consume and thieves break through and steal. ..."[3]

Power does not occupy the center but briefly; we are eventually replaced. Success and prestige are two temporary "goods" with limited ability to satisfy.

Family at the center sounds right to so many, but families are always changing. Children grow up and make their own decisions, many of which trouble their parents. Or, a mate dies and the family is radically changed. Any person at the center subjects us to the threat of loss.

A vocation is maintained only as long as age and health permit. Serving the self never fully satisfies. Our hobbies finally become meaningless.

Sex in a lifetime will vary greatly in its significance; but at the center sex will corrupt us.

Education contributes much to life but is a means and not an end.

What about health that seems to be an obsession the older we get? Arthur Frank, professor of sociology at the University of Calgary, has much wisdom concerning illness and health. He suggests that bodily vulnerability is what we humans are, that in spite of our concern to keep healthy, "that as a species and as individuals, we may need to be ill."[4] In fact he suggests that illness may be a necessity in realizing all we can become as humans. After all, we can never cure our final illness leading to death. Our bodies and physical health are deteriorating and that is what it means to be human.

None of the above is lasting, eternal or absolute. The gods

finally fail us because neither one nor all can unify life. We desperately need the God above all the gods.

Where Is God?

Where is the One? The Commandment points toward the Hebrew's Shema: "Hear, O Israel: The Lord our God is one Lord; and you will love the Lord your God with all your heart, and with all your soul, and with all your might."[5]

Where is this One, the focus or center of life, the One we cannot do without? In two Gospels we find the story of the Gerasene demoniac, a man possessed by demons.[6] This is the way the inner conflicts of a person were described in that day. Jesus came to him and asked him his name. He cried out, "My name is Legion, for we are many!" This is often our state. We are torn apart by the many.

"You will have no other gods before me." Where is the One? Look at the times when we call the name of God. I expect that we use the term not to establish that God exists, or to describe or explain God's nature. We cry "God!" or think God or are reaching out to God in negative or positive moments of meaning. The reaching out may be a cry in times of need, a whisper in times of anxiety, a song in times of joy, an alleluia in moments of thanks-giving, a protest in times of danger, a longing in times of reflection, or a curse in times of anger.

God is the mysterious, unshakable ground of what is; the center and depth of our lives, of human fellowship, of reality as a whole; the final and supreme authority upon which everything depends; that which is opposite us, beyond our control, and the source of our responsibility. God is greater than our minds or hearts. We cannot reduce the One to our small concepts or feelings. Life is greater than our life, history greater than our history, experience greater than our experience, and God is greater than our thinking or feeling level.

To fulfill the Commandment is to love this center, the way life is, and to trust in the One. One and only One leads me out of slavery to the many. One has set me free to live. One loves and accepts me no matter what. One meets me in good and evil, joy and sorrow, health and sickness, life and death. When this One is at the center of life, or, to say this another way, when unbounded love is at the center, all the gods are kept in their relative positions. The key to this Commandment is being absolutely related to the absolute and relatively related to all the relative "goods." What this means can be illustrated by making a few changes in the diagram on page 9.

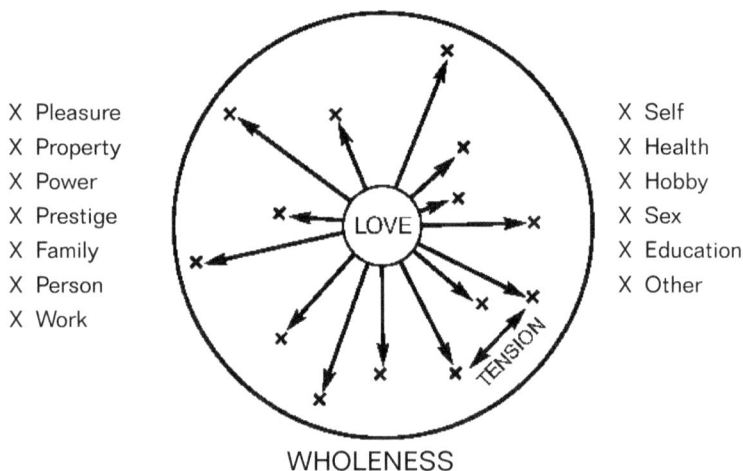

X Pleasure		X Self
X Property	LOVE	X Health
X Power		X Hobby
X Prestige		X Sex
X Family		X Education
X Person	TENSION	X Other
X Work		

WHOLENESS

Instead of the center being open territory subject to being possessed by one or more of the "goods," this diagrammed individual is so aware of being loved that she can relate to the relativities of life out of a fullness of love. The various "goods" are kept in relative relationships. Some inevitable tensions arise but this is different from that struggle to possess one's soul. Being absolutely related to the absolute keeps us relatively related to the relativities of life. "You will have no other gods before me."

God Is Presence

Who is sufficient for this? Not by ourselves! This One comes to us, is always coming; and we see that coming in Jesus of Nazareth. This God was not self-revealed as a powerful other: unapproachable, omniscient, and omnipotent. Instead, God came in a man empty of divinity (Paul in Philippians 2:7). God in Jesus shares life, promises life, preserves life and is everywhere the lover of life. To know God is to live. "God is life," says Leo Tolstoi, "everywhere of it, in it, and with it." God is everywhere life-giver and lover. This is the Presence that we can experience.

Where now do we see what was in Jesus? In the faces of those human beings about us! The worship of God involves devotion to one another and the needs of humanity present and future. God has, in the Christian affirmation, entered creation and identified with humanity, with our world. The God dimension disclosed in Jesus is in this world and not away from us.

This means that God can be hurt, thwarted, temporarily defeated, yet always rising again to be life-giver and lover. Nikos Kazantzakis, in a very provocative book entitled *The Saviors of God* has expressed this in these words: "My God ... struggles, for He is in peril every moment; he trembles and stumbles in every living thing, and He cries out. He is defeated incessantly, but rises again, full of blood and earth, to throw himself into battle once more. He is full of wounds, his eyes are filled with fear and stubbornness, his jawbones and temples are splintered. But He does not surrender, He ascends; He ascends with his feet, his hands, wiping his lips, undaunted."[7]

Death and resurrection, finding self by losing self, is built into the structure of life. Christians proclaim that God came to us in the man Jesus and thereby became our God. People ask, "Where is God?" No place out there. God is here, a part of life, and reflected in those about us. In John, Jesus said, "Whoever has seen me, has seen the Father."[8] And who is this "me"? "Inasmuch as you have done this to the least of them, you have done it to me." Inasmuch as you have seen the least of these, you have seen me. Inasmuch as you have given yourself to others, you have given yourself to me. This Presence can be experienced in the midst of living with the various relativities of life without being fully identified with any one.

This is the light of God that was in Jesus and why Christians call him Christ. This is the Presence and Power at work in us. By his gracious work, we live not scattered among the many but rooted in that one source of love from which we cannot be separated. The One keeps the many rightly related.

"You will have no other gods before me."

Notes
1. To avoid the awkward "he/she" or the incorrect "they," I will alternate the use of he and she throughout.
2. Goethe.
3. Matt. 6:19.
4. From Frank, *The Renewal of Generosity: Illness, Medicine, and How to Live*, and reprinted in "The Chronicle of Higher Eduction, 8/13/04
5. Deuteronomy 6:4.
6. Mark 5:1-10; Luke 8:26-31.
7. Simon and Schuster, New York, 1960 (paperback), pg. 103.
8. John 14:9

QUESTIONS FOR REFLECTION OR DISCUSSION

1. The author contends that we all have a tendency toward polytheism. What does that mean?
2. According to one definition, religion is ultimate concern. What is your ultimate concern, that which mainly occupies your mind and heart?
3. How do you understand idolatry?
4. What "gods" would you add to the author's list?
5. What is the difference between God and the gods?
6. How does God save us from selling our souls to any one or more of the gods?
7. What is the difference between an absolute good and a relative good. Is there an absolute good? If so, what is it? If not, what does that mean for life?

II

Nothing But a Reminder

You will not make for yourself an idol....

Who or what is God? People through the centuries have wrestled with this question finding no simple answer. God has been named, classified, and located again and again but always seems to break out of the assigned molds. The term "God" has had such varied use as to lead Paul Tillich to long for a moratorium on the word for a generation or two. Supreme Being is too nebulous to be satisfactory as a classification. And "dwelling in heaven" is so abstract and remote as to remove God from meaningful relationship with us. Who or what is God?

Let us come at this question as the Hebrew did and eliminate all that is not God. The first two Commandments direct us. In the previous chapter, we considered, "You will have no other gods before me." All that we trust in to give life meaning is less than God: pleasure, possessions, family, some person, job, education, or what-have-you. All are less than God; but we are still tempted to make one or another the end of life. This First Commandment lifts up the unity of God. He is the one and only. "The Lord our God is one Lord."

God Is Nothing.

The Second Commandment adds another dimension: "You will not make for yourself an idol." God is nothing. If this sounds shocking, try it this way: God is no thing; God cannot be positioned or located. This means much more than we might think.

The Second Commandment is an injunction against idolatry, which is much more than the primitive practice of making figures and bowing down before them. Idolatry is still with us, though in a somewhat disguised form. We still set up our mental images. Worshiping an unseen and unidentifiable God is hard. This was an age-long struggle with the Hebrews. We see, in the Hebrew Scriptures, that early effort to separate God from things. Moses caught the vision, though how is a great mystery. He had come from Egypt where the gods were formed and identified. Other people spoke of their gods and had figures in their minds. The Hebrews had no figure and no image.

Others made their sacrifices before idols, but the Hebrews sent their sacrificial smoke up into the skies. How much abuse they must have received! Where is your God? What does She look like? And the people often faltered. When Moses was away, they beseeched Aaron, "... make us gods, who will go before us...."[1] In other words, make us something that we can see and handle. Later, after the division of the kingdom, Israel to the north set up two golden calves at the center of worship.

The rank and file did not understand nor comprehend a God who is no thing. They wanted God objectified. Moses and the later prophets fought the battle. It was not until the exile that the people caught the vision. In Babylonian exile, surrounded by idols, they remembered their worship at the temple with its empty Holy of Holies and marveled at the mystery of the One who could not be captured in any form. The antagonism of the Hebrews toward any idol became a wonder of the ancient world. The Roman Empire gave the Hebrews a special dispensation. They did not have to bow down before idols. Other people did obeisance before the images of gods and emperors, but the Hebrews, never! It took them one thousand years of struggle; but once they embraced this truth, they could not forget it: God is no thing.

One of the greatest of religious insights is symbolized by the ancient Hebrew worship. To penetrate to the most secret heart of the temple, to the Holy of Holies, was to find emptiness. Nothing was there because God is no thing. How natural to want to have a God we can see, use, and manipulate for our purposes! This idolatry is still present today. We want to locate God and say that God is here or there. In this way we determine God's nature and character. We say that God is in the religious sphere of life; God is with the Church and church-like activities. God is in the sanctuary, and we go to church to meet God.

The truth is that God is not basically in the sanctuary but out in the world. We speak about faith and life in the sanctuary so that we are encouraged to live the life of faith outside. We speak about God in the gathered church so that we can recognize God's activity when we are scattered. God is nothing, no thing. God cannot be located. classified, and pigeon-holed. Neither can God be identified with any symbol.

God's Nature Guarded

More than this, the Commandment suggests that God's nature and activity are guarded jealously. Listen to the whole of the Second Commandment: "You will not make yourself an idol, whether in the form of anything that is in heaven above, or that is on the earth beneath, or that is in the water under the earth. You will not bow down to them or worship them; for I the Lord your God am a jealous God, punishing children for the iniquity of parents, to the third and fourth generation of those who reject me, but showing steadfast love to the thousandth generation of those who love me and keep my commandments."[2]

This has always been a hard word to understand. A jealous God punishing generations is an Hebraic and human way of speaking about God. The terms are not absolute, but they point in the right direction. Apostasy and idolatry cost. The punishment is conflict. As someone has said, "Make some thing your god, and it will plague you like the devil." The character of our god will determine our character. God's jealousy integrates life; God demands total devotion with nothing withheld. A jealous God will not tolerate reverence that is due to God to be ascribed to another.

This brings us to all the mental images toward which we focus our lives. We are image collectors: a house, a car, a degree, an office or position, a ranch, a place at the lake. What is the image for you that remains in your mind as the focal point of interest and concern? We serve our image by sacrificing our character and the welfare of others to realize it. Having achieved the "right" relationship to our image, we bask in its glory. But God renders meaningless the images we work so hard to make into realities. Too soon the sweetness melts away and in its place is the acid taste of emptiness and boredom. The making of images to which we give the devotion of our lives is an exercise in futility.

Yet, there is so much good in the world: so many things for which we can work; so much beauty, joy, and delight in creation! The key is not selling our souls to acquire or to create. Considering now the latter, the Hebrew took this Commandment to be an injunction against all sculpture and painting, all the plastic arts. Jews have, for the most part, limited their aesthetic pursuits. They have accomplished much in literature, music, and religion but have lacked the aesthetic sense in formative arts. This is illustrated in Chaim Potok's novel, *My Name Is Asher Lev*. The young son of devoutly religious Jews has painting skills that are frowned upon by his parents. The novel builds up the tension over his artistry to a tragic state of separation. Painting was for the parents tantamount to idolatry.

The book of Exodus is barren of a sense of the majesty of the desert or the beauty of a sunrise. Paul traveled through some of the most beautiful country in the world, but not even a blade of grass is mentioned in his letters. The Hebrews went too far, perhaps, in guarding against nature worship as well as the worship of human creations. They demanded no representation at all. They held to a God revealed not in some static image but in the ambiguities of a dynamic and moving history.

This Commandment attempts to protect God from being

used for our purposes. The what and where of God's presence and involvement in human life is kept in a state of mystery. With our images we try to take divinity into our own power, to manipulate reality, to control life, and to determine the meaning and purpose of life. At the heart of this prohibition of images is the realization that when God is identified with any representation, we exclude God from our relationship with our brothers and sisters. An image puts God, the meaning-giver, into a category beyond us and thereby avoids the human problems. We have God at our disposal and control. This is true of all idolatry, including bibliolatry which replaces the living God of history by a book or part of a book. During the controversy about placing the Ten Commandments in public places and the intensity with which many insist that the Commandments be there, I recall seeing a cartoon. A marble monument of the Ten was the focus and a character at the side exclaimed, "Hey, wait a minute! Isn't the Second Commandment You will make no graven image ?" (idol in NRSV)

An amazing story in Exodus has Moses pleading to see God's face.[3] He wanted an image. In the dialogue with God, created by a great theological story-teller centuries after Moses, God makes it clear that there can be no view of God directly. However, God allows Moses to position himself in a cleft of a rock where he is prevented from seeing God until after God passes by. Only then can he see God's backside. One Hebrew scholar says that the Hebrew word means buttocks. A pastor friend preached a sermon on this text and entitled it "God the Streaker." The meaning is clear. God can be seen only after the fact, an intimation of Presence, but not directly.

Without images we are most likely to meet God and be truly open to God in whatever and wherever God is.

Only One Image

There are no images of God, except that one that God has created. God has made a self-image against God's own law prohibiting images. "So God created humankind in his image, in the image of God he created them; male and female he created them."[4]

God is invisible, but we have problems living without God, so God created for us a reminder, an image. The meaning of being human is to be a reminder of God. To look at human beings at their best is to be reminded of something eternal, loving, and self-giving. To know what this means, we have a revelation. Behold the man! "For it is the God who said, 'Let light shine out of darkness,' who has shown in our hearts to give the light of the knowledge of the glory of God in the face of Jesus Christ."[5]

Jesus' vocation was to represent God. What a fearful calling: to play God, to live God, to be God to others in suffering and serving love! In being the reminder of God, Jesus did not lord it over others. He was open to people. His anger was never toward people in need. Whether they were prostitutes, foreigners, tax collectors, adulterers, maimed, lepers, or other marginalized parts of society, Jesus responded to them in love. His anger was reserved for the scribe and the self-righteous Pharisee whose religion was the book. By being present to the neighbor, Jesus revealed the reality of God not in images but in loving deeds. He was and is the Presence of God in human life.

The struggle goes on. No images or pictures to worship, no creations of our minds and hearts, no face or form. Our primary calling is to reproduce, by God's help, the mind and character of the man Jesus in our own lives. At our best, we are nothing but a reminder; but this is enough for God's activity to remain in life.

"You will not make for yourself an idol. . . ."

Notes
1. Exodus 32:1b
2. Exodus 20:4-6
3. Exodus 33:18 ff
4. Genesis 1:27
5. 2 Corinthians 4:6

QUESTIONS FOR REFLECTION OR DISCUSSION

1. What can you not live without?
2. Have you ever lost a "god" and been utterly devastated?
3. Can you imagine creating something that would become too precious?
4. How are we tempted to locate God?
5. How would you respond to someone's asking, "Where is your God?"
6. What problems do you have with an unseen and unidentifiable God?
7. How do you feel about Warner Sallman's "Head of Christ" or some other representation of Jesus being the focal point of a worship area?
8. How do you relate to being the image of God?

III

What's in a Name?

*You will not make wrongful use of the
name of the Lord your God....*

In the Introduction we affirmed that our relationship to God does not begin by following the law. First, God acts to establish the relationship. In the Hebrew Scriptures, a loving and caring God delivers the Hebrews from slavery. In the Christian Scriptures, the God of love establishes a new people through the Jesus story. In both cases people respond in gratitude to what God has done and learn together how to love God and to love the neighbor. The Commandments point to the right response.

In the previous chapters we considered the first two of the Ten Commandments. First, "You will have no other gods before me." But we find ourselves scattered among the many. We are pulled in many directions by pleasure, goods, family, work, and many other aspects of life. But God is one and cannot be identified with any part of God's creation. In the Jesus event we see that One revealed who puts in right relationship the many.

The Second, "You will not make for yourself a graven image." God cannot be located. God is no thing. God's image is only found in the human beings God has created. We see this image most clearly in Jesus of Nazareth and because of him, we see the image of God in others.

Faithfully wrestling with the Commandments promises to help form our lives. This is not simply knowing them and not merely obeying them legalistically. We are both free from them and free for them. We are to take the Commandments seriously, if not absolutely. They do not establish our relationship with God; they are responses to the right relationship that is given by God. So it is with the Third Commandment to which we now turn.

What's in a Name?

"You will not make wrongful use of the name of the Lord your God...." What's in a name? Shakespeare said, "A rose by any other name would smell as sweet." This may be true about roses, but there is more in a name than we might think. Many have thought this to be a minor Commandment. It could not be too serious. Perhaps the improper use of the name could be crude, distasteful, but hardly a grievous wrong. What else is involved with a name?

Knowing a name is to have some control over a relationship. Moses, upon sensing the call to go to Egypt, wanted to know God's name. The name, in the biblical story, was not given to him. All he knew was that "I am" was sending him, or that being itself was behind the call. God was not to be under the control of Moses or anyone. Knowing a name is a control factor.

An illustration of this occurred to me following a jogging experience. Each morning on my route a dog from one house would come barking after me. One day an adult from the house was in the yard; and when the dog came after me, she called, "Pepper, come here!" The dog obeyed. Another morning Pepper came after me again and I cried out, "Pepper, No!" Pepper turned around and went back to his yard. I had found a control factor.

Yet another more human experience happened when I was at a reception. Being a bit bored, I went to the hostess to ask the name of a stranger across the room. Having a name, I went up to the man and greeted him. "Hello, Dave, how good to see you. How are things going?" I could see the blank look and the confusion on his face. He did not know me. Who was in control of that immediate situation? After a few moments, I confessed my ruse, and we had a laugh together.

Knowing a name usually means having a relationship. What is our relationship to the one named God? The name is part of the one who bears it, and the bearer is present in some mysterious way in the name. Call out a name in your mind, and that person appears before you. For the Hebrew, knowing the Divine name was to have the power of the Divine for blessing and cursing.

The Hebrew people thought that God's name was revealed for purposes of worship. The prohibition of this Commandment was an attempt to protect the Divine name from abuse. Using the Lord's name in vain is using it lightly, without proper regard and thereby making it meaningless. As God is holy, separate from creation, so God's name is holy.

The Jews came to feel that the personal name for God could not be pronounced. It was too sacred and subject to being misused. We think that this personal name was Yahweh. Other names were used as substitutes: Adonai, Elohim, El Shaddai (translated Lord, God, and God Almighty). Jehovah is a mistake; there is no such name. It was accidentally formed from taking the consonants of the personal name and using the vowels of another. They were put together by the ancient scribes to remind readers not to pronounce the personal name but to use the substitute suggested by the vowel markings placed under the consonants.

Such a careful use of the name is perhaps too much for us. On the other hand, we use the name so lightly that we lose reverence in the process. If we have an awareness of the mystery that is God, are sensitive to that Other who has brought us into being, and experience from time to time a Presence, reverence is the consequence.

The Commandment forbids a cheap and easy use of the Divine name to cover up poverty of thought or feeling. To use the name lightly, to curse or swear, is no mark of intelligence; it takes no brains; and it is not smart or funny. Cursing is used primarily by inarticulate people to impress others but becomes a crude habit that reveals the impotence and weakness of the user.

Punishments and consequences come from profanity. The result is inevitably irreverence. One will not be struck by lightning or suffer some sudden catastrophe, but consequences do follow. The high places of life are leveled; nothing is sacred. Our idea of God and appreciation of God's loving activities will wane and in the process some of the finest influences of life.

How could it be otherwise? Use the name of some loved one without affection and appreciation, and soon real love and respect are gone. No one speaks irreverently of what is loved. The Hebrews exercised extreme care in the use of God's name. They called on the name, prophesied in the name, blessed the name, praised the name, trusted in the name, and sought refuge in the name. But they were fearful of any misuse of the name of God.

The Nature In The Name

So far this has been the common view of this Commandment. But more is at stake. The name in the Bible is more than a designation. The name has to do with the character and basic nature of what is named. And what is the nature of God?

When Moses asked for God's name, he was not given a personal name that could be identified. He was told, "I AM WHO I AM ... say to the Israelites, 'I am has sent me to you.'"[1] This "I am" is the God of Abraham and Sarah, Isaac and Rebecca, and Jacob and Rachel. God is the "is-ness" of life, what really is, and not what appears to be. God is the reality behind all that is.

This Commandment was warring against a magical world view. The Hebrew was opposed to all incantations, sorcery, and other magical uses of the name where by repetition the user thought he was gaining power.

The Commandment was also a reminder that God was not to be identified with anything that lacks reality or truth, not to be connected with falsehood or deceit. In that ancient day, this meant something about oath-taking. To swear by God's name was to call on God as a witness for truth, which assumes that a person would lie otherwise. In that day, an elaborate system of oath-taking prevailed. Confidence in the veracity of something asserted depended upon what you swore by. One could swear by heaven, by earth, by Jerusalem, by one's own head. Some oaths were more binding than others. Using God's name was the most binding for God was to be associated only with truth, with the way things are.

We need to go past oath-taking to respect what is. To be God's people is to have no traffic with falsehood. Matthew records Jesus as saying, "Again you have heard that it was said to those of ancient times, 'You will not swear falsely, but will carry out the vows you have made to the Lord.' But I say to you, Do not swear at all, either by heaven, for it is the throne of God, or by the earth, for it is his footstool, or by Jerusalem, for it is the city of the great King. And do not swear by your head, for you cannot make one hair white or black. Let your word be 'Yes, Yes' or 'No, No'; anything more than this comes from the evil one."[2]

The Christian is to be rooted in what is. Words are to be used to point to the truth. Is this so? Religion for many is associated with good feelings acquired from the repetition of certain well-loved phrases and the denunciation of those who do not use them. Each pastor is tempted to cater to the urge of his congregation to hear over and over again certain phrases which are supposed to be the guarantee of soundness of faith. Here are some: "faith of our fathers," "Bible-believing Christians," "God-fearing," "saved by the blood of Christ." You can add some others. What do such words mean? This takes struggle. What is of God needs to point to reality, the way life is, and not deceive.

Naming A Control Factor

The main way we break this Commandment is in our attempt to humanize or domesticate God. An article I read compared our treatment of dogs and our treatment of God. We are always perverting the relationship. We tend to make dogs human, which is bad for dogs. They are forced into an unnatural, human mode of existence. It is a de-caninization for dogs to be treated as humans. No dog can be the significant other. People become human in relationship to their own kind, not in relationship to an animal. On the other hand, we try to domesticate God. We want to make God usable and functional. "My God and I go to the fields together as good friends often do." That is domestication! God is wonder and mystery and is only reflected to us through others. Our life is found in relationship to our own kind, each of whom reflects God's nature to us. We cannot make God human. God makes God's self human by coming to us through others. The significance of every other relationship is derived from our relationship to God. Every other is an object of God's love; therefore, we cannot despise or treat lightly any other. Every other is the possible channel for the love of God to us.

The reality of God is what is revealed in the man Jesus. His nearness is not given in nature except indirectly; God does not place God's self at our disposal. God is established in the human scene of history by choice. We would not know this except that God enters the human scene to free us from anything in life that would enslave us. In Jesus we see one who was free. He reached out for life and more life in every experience. Life was always ahead, always becoming. This is evident even during the crucifixion.

I had a Spirit experience some time ago watching the television program, "Arthur Rubinstein at 90." For years he has been for me both an artistic and a spirit genius. He was asked by the interviewer, "Do you believe in God?" After a pause he said, "Not the man with the beard." He affirmed belief in the mystery behind life, the mystery of the way life is. He was asked about his comment in the first volume of his memoirs about being the happiest of men. "What is the source of your happiness?" He said that his happiness was born after a suicide attempt at age 20. He had arrived at a zero hour in his life. In a hotel room in Berlin, without money, and with the woman he desired committed to another, he tried to strangle himself. The cords broke. In frustration he played the piano awhile and then walked into the night and was born again. The word came to him: "Fool! Life does not depend on the amount of money you have or having the woman of your desire. Life is always in front of you." This is the Jesus word. Call it by whatever name you will. This Polish-American Jew had heard the Good News. This is what is revealed to us in the Jesus story and is why Christians call Jesus "Christ" which in essence means the activity of God.

To be Christian, Paul says, is to do everything in the name of the Lord Jesus;[3] that is, in the nature and character of what is revealed in him. And what has been revealed is that reality can be trusted. Love is in life; therefore, I do not have to use magic, incantation, sorcery, or even the repetition of familiar words and phrases to find life. I don't even have to obey the laws. I will use the law, civil or religious, as the accumulated wisdom of the ages. I will seek right relationships out of gratitude for what God is doing for me. But my loyalty and allegiance is not to any law but to the living activity of God.

Life is given to me again and again and is always ahead. This is God's doing. God's nature and character are revealed in the midst of life. Experiencing the wonder, mystery, and love of God, I will try by this grace to take seriously the Commandment:

"You will not make wrongful use of the name of the Lord your God. . . ."

Notes
1. Exodus 3:14
2. Matt. 5:33-37
3. Colossians 3:17

QUESTIONS FOR REFLECTION OR DISCUSSION

1. What is important about a name?

2. What is the difference between a name today and the name in the biblical period?
3. How is knowing a name a control factor?
4. Doing something in the name of Jesus means what?
5. Do we really know the name of God?

IV

The Rhythm of Life

Remember the sabbath day, and keep it holy.

Sunday is still the day of the week when somewhere around 50 million people in our country gather to worship God. The Fourth Commandment tells us, "Remember the sabbath day, to keep it holy." Is that what many of us are doing? Again, we are taking a new look at the Ten Commandments to see what the word is for us.

This ancient decalogue has been a factor in the age-long process of humanizing life, making life more for us. The consciousness of one God has led to the concept of one world and one humanity. Reverence and respect for life and the reality behind it are inspired by this ancient word.

The Ten Commandments are amazing in their lack of national prejudice or racial peculiarities. Even the Fourth Commandment, which on the surface seems so Jewish, is more than a parochial statement. "Remember (or observe) the sabbath day, to keep it holy." No other commandment has had such an effect upon our social life and thought. A day set apart from other days, kept holy, is still a part of our social fabric. We know this as much in the neglect as in the observance. This special day cries out for attention.

Sabbath for Humanity

The observance of the sabbath is not for God's sake but for the welfare of humanity. The authority and sanctity of the institution of this special day come from its service to a wide variety of human needs. In Jesus' word, "The sabbath was made for humankind, not humankind for the sabbath. . . ."[1]

How is this day for us, for humanity? Exodus and Deuteronomy both have the Ten Commandments. The Fourth has the greatest difference between them. Exodus says: "Remember the sabbath day, and keep it holy. Six days you will labor, and do all your work; but the seventh day is a sabbath to the Lord your God; you will not do any work, you, your son, or your daughter, your male or your female slave, your livestock, or the alien resident in your towns. For in six days the Lord made heaven and earth, the sea, and all that is in them, but rested the seventh day; therefore the Lord blessed the sabbath day and consecrated it."

A day of rest? Why? Because God rested on the seventh day! Six days for labor and one for rest. In this word the Hebrew tied the sabbath observance to the act of creation, to the structure of the universe. The sabbath day is not just a Jewish ordinance beginning at Sinai; it is written into creation itself from the beginning. Work and rest are part of the nature and activity of God. We do not have to hold to a literal seven day creation to see this truth. All of life is involved in the rhythm of work and rest.

Deuteronomy's approach is different: "Observe the sabbath day and keep it holy, as the Lord your God commanded you. Six days you will labor, and do all your work; but the seventh day is a sabbath to the Lord your God; you will not do any work—you, or your son, or your daughter, or your male or female slave, or your ox, or your donkey, or any of your livestock, or the resident aliens in your towns, so that your male and female slave may rest as well as you. Remember that you were a slave in the land of Egypt, and the Lord our God brought you out from there with a mighty hand and an outstretched arm; therefore the Lord your God commanded you to keep the sabbath day."

In this account the Hebrew was reminded that he was a slave in the land of Egypt before he knew freedom. In Egypt, he had no rest from slave labor. He was admonished to see that those who worked for him were not so burdened. His relationship to his neighbor was to be based on gratitude for what God has done for him. He was being told, "You are free. Now do what is necessary for your neighbor to be free from the toil that knows no rest." From the beginning rest was a part of life. Social responsibility means to provide for rest. The rhythm of work and rest is the way life was meant to be. Remember, observe! And the Hebrews did and elaborated upon the whole idea until the sabbath became a burden and not a blessing. The real purpose was hidden in a mass of regulations. Jesus came and with amazing freedom overlooked the maze of legalistic proscriptions and concentrated on human need.

Jesus and his disciples were walking through a field one day. The disciples plucked some grain and ate it. Normally this would have been all right. The custom was to allow a hungry traveler to gather a handful or two of grain, but not on the sabbath. The disciples had broken four of 39 tasks considered work: reaping, winnowing, threshing, and preparing a meal. The Pharisees protested, "Look! Why are they doing what is not lawful on the sabbath?"[2] Jesus reminded them of how David with some of his friends ate the bread offered to God. The shewbread consisted of 12 loaves placed on the table before the Holy of Holies. These were replaced once a week. By law only the priests were allowed to eat the bread.

Jesus drove home the point already mentioned: "The sabbath was made for man, not man for the sabbath." The Pharisees' religion was all ritual and obeying rules, laws, and regulations. Jesus broke these freely. The law was subordinate to human need. If the good of human beings was furthered by violating the law, then a lower law was broken to keep a higher one. Bodily needs took priority over sabbath laws. For Jesus the sabbath was given as a help, not a burden. The intention was to make life better and fuller, not to restrict it.

Legalistic minds through the centuries have made the sabbath a burden and not a blessing. So with the Christian Sunday.

The Jewish sabbath (Saturday) was replaced by the resurrection day. Early Christians tried to observe both the Jewish sabbath and Christian Sunday; but by the fourth century, Saturday was replaced by Sunday.

Meaning Today

What does all this mean for us in the twenty-first century? Rest and refreshment are still basic needs. Common sense tells us that we cannot go at the same pace seven days a week without suffering. And many of us are living at that pace.

In many major cities, Sunday is a shopping day. An MIT professor sees this as a diminishing of the family. He acknowledges that an oppressive Sunday piety can be narcotic and insincere. Yet, it did affirm the possibility of human relationships. The market sweeps all before it. The rhythm of life is gone, and capitalism has moved in to capture all space and time. He called this Sunday imperialism.

The French years ago tried to abolish Sunday, and it led to disaster. Such a special day goes back as far as recorded history. In ancient Babylonia, a "day of quieting the heart" was recognized. We have the same need for a day uncomplicated by our competitive places in the world of work and social striving. We need a day to help us remember who we are.

I am not advocating a return to the legalism of nineteenth century Christianity. We have gone through a period in which Christianity was going to church, reading the Bible, saying grace, having family worship, and keeping a strict observance of Sunday. But piety could, at the same time, be deaf to the call of need and blind to the tears of the world.

The best way to use religious disciplines is to help people. The final arbiter in the use of all things is love and not law. For Jesus, the most important thing was not obedience to the law, but the spontaneous answer to the cry of need. Persons are more important than laws. People matter more than systems. The best worship of God is to do good to people, and doing good to people includes doing good to one's self.

Rhythm of Life

How do we get this rhythm of life? How can we remember to have a special day and see that others do, too? What do we need? *The New York Times* has a travel section that ran a feature entitled "How to Chase the Weekend Blues." The writer says that statistics show that depression is most severe on weekends, that suicides are more numerous. The advice she gives is to go to museums, schedule diversions, hike, weave, learn a sport, and don't try to solve marital problems on weekends. Avoid stimulants and depressants, and, incidentally, go to church. Her prescription is to structure life. She is right.

We are physical creatures. The observance of a special day means a change of pace. For a manual laborer, a day of rest. For a white-collar worker, outside exercise. All need refreshment. This will mean different things to different people.

One we often forget is mother if the mother is the home-maker. Even though new patterns of family life are much in vogue today, many traditional homes still have mother busy on Sunday: washing, dressing, serving breakfast, preparing children for church school and worship, and fixing dinner. How does she hear that hymn, "O Day of Rest and Gladness?" Did you notice that the Fourth Commandment in both Exodus and Deuteronomy said nothing about mother resting? Perhaps they were too realistic for that. The servants and the cattle were mentioned, but not mother. Yet, she needs the change of pace, too, and the rest of us are responsible for seeing that she gets it sometime. (Another interpretation for the absence of mother is that the Commandment was directed to both father and mother.)

Out of gratitude for our deliverance from burdensome toil grows concern for our neighbors as well as ourselves. Each one needs a change in the physical pace of life. But we are more than physical. We have minds as well. If we do physical work all week, Sunday is a good time for reading. If we read all week, our minds should be at rest on Sunday. Conversations with family and friends are in order on Sunday if such is denied us during the week. Each must decide the need. If Sunday is out for this change of pace, another day should be chosen. We need the rhythm. Our need takes priority over any sabbath law.

Religious Activities

So far, I have had a minimal reference to church activities; but this dimension is present in the Commandment, also. We are spiritual creatures who need constantly a check on our purposes and perspectives. We desperately need time for reflection, the cultivation of the higher values, and attention to the spirit dimension of life. Is this the way it is? Or is it more like this anonymous poem that I committed to memory years ago:

> This is the age
> Of the half-read page,
> And the quick hash
> And the mad dash.
> The bright night
> With the nerves tight.
> The plane hop
> And a brief stop.
> The lamp tan in a short span.
> The big shot in a good spot.
> And the brain strain,
> And the heart pain,
> And the cat naps
> Till the spring snaps
> —And the fun's done.

This bit of doggerel is too close for comfort. A word of judgment is found in this crass humor. To the measure of truth found here, the Church provides a corrective role. The rhythm of life involves body, mind, and spirit. Busyness, without reflective time, is unhealthy. If our choice is always rush, rush to the neglect of caring for the total self, we will suffer the consequences. But no conflict is necessary. This special day offers many hours, and worship is a crucial part of the rhythm.

Our worship life can lead to a cleansing of our imaginations by God's beauty, a quickening of consciences by God's holiness, a nourishment of minds by God's truth, and a redirecting of our lives by God's purpose. We can structure ourselves to get the rhythm right instead of worshiping our work, working at our play, and playing at our worship. Work is to be enjoyed bringing us satisfaction; play is to give us relaxation and refreshment; and worship serves to focus our minds and hearts on the truths of life.

A special day, a different day, is needed by each one of us. The call is to plan for ourselves and make it possible for others, for our sakes and for their sakes. "The sabbath was made for man, not man for the sabbath."

Somewhere I read that rabbis taught that the purpose of sabbath was threefold. The first was to free the poor as well as the rich for at least one day a week, and that included the animals, too. Nobody had to take an order from anyone on the sabbath. The second was to give people time to evaluate their work as God evaluated creation to see if their work, too, is really life-giving. And the third reason for the sabbath was to give people a space to contemplate the real meaning of life. If anything has brought the modern world to the brink of destruction, it must surely be the loss of the concept of sabbath observance.

"Remember the sabbath day, and keep it holy."

Notes
1. Mark 2:27
2. Mark 2:24

Questions for Reflection or Discussion

1. What is the difference between the sabbath and Sunday?
2. In what way is the sabbath Sunday?
3. Why is Sunday for us?
4. How can Sunday be a burden?
5. What is the main benefit of observing Sunday?
6. Does our contemporary life call for a less legalistic observance of Sunday?
7. What is the meaning of Sunday observance for today?

V
Honor and Respect

Honor your father and your mother....

So far the Commandments have focused us on the God relationship. Now we are led to consider our relationship to others, especially our parents. This relationship is more than obedience to some law. An ethic based on law leads either to self-righteousness as we take pride in our accomplishments and build up our list of good deeds; or, the law leads us to despair by showing us how far short we have fallen. To paraphrase Paul: The good we ought to do, we haven't; and what we ought not to do, we have.

Yet, the law is important: "dikes of love in a loveless world," one author writes. The law is a guide, a tool, a help when love is not sure of itself. Behind the law is a loving Presence. Love, God's universal love, binds us to others and leads us to acts of love. Without love the law is an intolerable burden. With love that comes from the awareness of a loving Presence, the law is an aid to love's expression. The story of what love requires is the story of ethics as seen from the perspective of faith. The Ten Commandments, the ethical decalogue, represents a people's experience with a love that leads them to an answering love to God and neighbor. This takes a special focus in the fifth Commandment: "Honor your father and your mother."

The Bridge Commandment

This is the transitional Commandment. So far we have considered our religious duties, the expression of love to God: no worshiping other gods, no attempting to capture God in time or place, dealing seriously with the way life is, and giving due consideration to the God-given rhythm of rest and work. Each of the first four is an expression of the love for God. Commandments six to ten have to do with moral duties, or our relationship to other human beings.

"Honor your father and your mother" is the bridge to what follows. Father and mother are among the people to whom we relate. At the same time, our relationship to our parents is in a special way a God-given relationship. God's claim on every life comes through the parent relationship. Life is a gift, as is the image in us of the Divine. That gift and image, and the breath of life itself, are transmitted to us through father and mother. The life which parents bear and give us is God's life.

The holiness of God is upheld in the honoring of father and mother. How mysterious the whole process is! Fathers and mothers play a part, but the result is not something which parents predetermine. Each individual is unique and different; but our uniqueness is not by parental order but by a Divine ordering. Parents represent the mystery of our existence. In spite of their weakness and failings, they have been the channels to the mystery of God.

To honor father and mother involves reverence. To honor is to prize highly, to show respect to, to glorify and exult. Nuances of caring and showing affection are in all of these. To honor is a term used to describe the relationship to God and is part of worship. Our parents are visible representations of God and exert authority on God's behalf. This Commandment is a transition or bridge between love of God and human love. Both are here with the conviction that a dishonoring of parents is a dishonoring of God.

Relationship Tensions

In spite of the given relationship, the link between the generations is often thin and sometimes breaks. Misunderstanding often creeps in between parents and children, the old and the young. This is the way life is. The young are working to establish their own lives, to find their own independence. They push out in independence and if successful are then willing to reach back and relate. The breaking of dependency ties is not a radical break but the change from one kind of relationship to another. The clashes of temperament are the prelude to the discovery of a new relationship as hearts are turned in a mature way to the parents.

So it has always been. The generations rarely understand each other. The Commandment says "honor" even though parents are not always understood. Tension does exist between parents and children. *The Prophet* by Gibran has this meaningful section on children:

> *Your children are not your children.*
> *They are the sons and daughters of Life's longing for itself.*
> *They come through you but not from you,*
> *And though they are with you yet they belong not to you.*
> *You may give them your love but not your thoughts.*
> *For they have their own thoughts.*
> *You may house their bodies but not their souls,*
> *For their souls dwell in the house of tomorrow, which you cannot visit,*
> *   not even in your dreams.*
> *You may strive to be like them, but seek not to make them like you.*
> *For life goes not backward nor tarries with yesterday.*
> *You are the bows from which your children as living arrows are sent*
> *   forth.*
> *The archer sees the mark upon the path of the infinite, and He bends*
> *   you with His might that His arrows may go swift and far.*
> *Let your bending in the archer's hand be for gladness;*
> *For even as he loves the arrow that flies, so He loves also the bow that*
> *   is stable.*
>
> —Kahlil Gibran

Our children are not ours; they did not ask to be born.

They will change physically, emotionally, and intellectually. Each time they enter the house following an absence they will be more independent. Be glad! Each time they return they will have more convictions. Be glad of that, too. Each time they come back we will discover some of our values modified or rejected. We can also rejoice in this.

They are not ours. They are the arrows, and we are the bows. The Archer uses us to send them forth. Hopefully, we will be bows that can be bent; but the bending is a strain, and sometimes involves pain as well. We have to work at being flexible. Recent insights reveal that the forces that shape children are (1) genes, (2) family, and (3) school room. We parents are second, which means we have to try harder.

Parenthood is an institution of God. Parents are God-substitutes. Infants or small children cannot distinguish between parents and God. Parents represent the Divine, the God-dimension, to their children. All through our lives our relationship to our parents has a close tie with our relationship to God. "Honor your father and your mother."

Aged Parents

Something else! This Commandment basically is a word about the relationship with aged parents. Some primitive societies pushed the elderly out to die in the elements. But Judaism and Christianity are family-centered and recognize the blessing in being related across generational lines.

The elderly live by memory instead of hope. Hope is of the future, and memory is of the past. The old must be taught to hope and to live for the future even while there is little left. But the young must be taught to look at the past of which they know nothing. The old look forward in imagination to what youth see; the young look back to discover what the old have already seen. When this happens, both are blessed.

Tension between the generations is part of the tragedy of life. The story of Romeo and Juliet is the story of such a tragedy. Romeo and Juliet are the young. The Montague and the

Capulet families represent the old. The tension and conflict form the substance of the drama, and the result is tragedy. We can see real life here. The old represent wisdom and earthbound experience. These are needed correctives to the soaring fantasies, untested idealism, and often despair of youth. But the idealism and the intensity of imagined possibilities are equally needed correctives to the stable and often cynical view of age. O, that we could turn our hearts to one another! How much this is needed!

The Promise

One thing more is needed. This is the Commandment with a promise. "Honor your father and your mother ... that your days may be prolonged, and that it may go well with you."

Our future state and continued happiness is bound to the right relationship to the authoritative influences on our lives. Martin Luther was right in seeing this Commandment as relating to all authority over us. To fulfill this Commandment out of gratitude for God's activity is to give willing obedience and whole hearted service to whatever is placed over us. Part of God's activity is to place us in authoritative structures.

The work of this Commandment is directed to our fleshly parents, to be sure; but also to our spiritual parent, the Church; the temporal parent, the state; and our vocational parents: managers, bosses, and whoever. More than fleshly parents are involved. A whole host of relationships call forth our honor and respect.

How can we do this? "In the Lord," in the understanding of the nature and character of Jesus whom we call Christ! He could feel and take animosity; and he could sense misunderstanding, yet continue to love. Whether or not we always understand our parents or our youth, they are loved and are part of the God-given nature of life. We love them "in the Lord." This is more than a feeling. Honoring comes before loving. Honoring is recognizing God's love and doing the acts of love until we discover in the process the presence of the One who turns the hearts of the parents to children, and the hearts of children to the parents.

The Fourth Commandment comes with a promise. Our lives and our well-being depend upon our response to God's love which comes to us through all our fathers and mothers.

"Honor your father and your mother...."

QUESTIONS FOR REFLECTION OR DISCUSSION

1. What is the relationship between God and parents?
2. What is the mystery of parenthood?
3. Why do tensions arise between children and parents?
4. Is there a different life focus between the young and the elderly?
5. How do the generations need each other?

VI
Reverence for Life

You will not murder.

Here we are alive again! We are dying every day; yet, here we are alive. Last night we slept; our bodies and minds rested in suspended animation. This morning we arose from the death of sleep to receive life again. Right now we are alive. We are sustained in our living. This state is not something that we earned. It comes as a gift. Life is a gift, moment by moment.

How do we express gratitude for life? This was the problem of the ancient Hebrews who found themselves free from the death of slavery. They had new life. Now, what were they to do about it? The Ten Commandments became the way that expressed gratitude for the gift of life. They were not the style of life for earning God's favor but a way of responding to God's grace.

This is the perspective we have been maintaining as we have looked at these Commandments. No other gods, no location of God, not taking the Lord's name in vain, keeping the sabbath day, and honoring father and mother are all expressions of gratitude. So it is with the next Commandment.

Killing in General

"You will not kill" in the older tranlations has now been

translated, "You will not murder." To the Hebrew, grateful for life, this meant no violent, unauthorized killing arising from feelings of hatred or malice. Life in the community of Israel was to be protected, and one Hebrew was not to kill another wantonly. But this Commandment was not applicable to animals. We see the word in Genesis: "Every moving thing that lives will be food for you. . . ."[1]

Neither was this Commandment applicable to enemies in war, suicides, capital punishment, nor blood revenge. In regard to revenge, the Hebrew was allowed to slay one who had killed his nearest kin, whether it was purposely or by accident. But the matter stopped there. Feuds and continuous revenge were not permitted. This was a great advance over unlimited vengeance practiced by most people of that day.

Yet, more must be said. The Hebrew understanding is not the last word on the subject. The Hebrew Scriptures present life as God's creation. Human life is the end product of God's creative activity in the evolutionary process. And Hebrew life is the most precious of all life. Christian Scriptures have a wider scope. New light is cast on the human relationship to all of life. The Christian receives the Scripture of the Jews but insists on reading it through the insight found in the Gospels.

To Jesus all life is sacred, because all life is of God. In the words of Jesus in the Gospel of Luke about sparrows: ". . . not one of them is forgotten in God's sight."[2] All of life shares in the great mystery of creation. Jesus used examples from the natural world to point to the activity of God: birds, flowers, trees, and seeds. A mystery is found at the heart of all living things. Alfred Lord Tennyson expressed it this way:

> *Flower in the crannied wall,*
> *I pluck you out of the crannies,*
> *I hold you here, root and all, in my hand, Little flower.*
> *But if I could understand*
> *What you are, root and all, and all in all,*
> *I should know what God and man is.*

We sense some poetic exaggeration here, but the truth still emerges. The whole world of nature, with its various forms of life involved in birth and death, is a mysterious but wonderful part of God's creation. Where else in this universe is life? The possibility remains that life is to be found only on this planet and nowhere else in the vast reaches of space, as far as we now know. We can lift up reverence for all of life in the Commandment, "You will not murder" or "kill" as in many translations.

The Natural World

What is our relationship to the natural world? Do we sense the mystery in every living creature? Perhaps the form of life that is least appreciated is the insect kingdom. Of what use are all the insects? We cannot answer this question completely. Yet, we do know some things. Insects do provide food for birds. They pollinate flowers and fruit trees and seem to be part of the balance of nature. In Jainism, a religion with a kinship to Buddhism, we find the conviction that no harm is to be brought to any creature. The Jains wear masks to guard against the act of breathing which may harm an insect. They sweep the path before them to prevent the possible stepping on some living creature.

Albert Schweitzer is known for his philosophy of reverence for life. To him, all life was one. Every creature depends on others, and all are entitled to respect and care. "You will not kill" meant for Schweitzer that no living plant or animal was to be killed needlessly. If necessary it was to be done with sorrow.

Schweitzer carried this philosophy into the life of his hospital and village. Animals were accorded a place of safety and arrangements encouraged them to live in peace with each other. A bee that had invaded the dining room would be caught gently, not killed, and released outside. When a column of ants invaded a visitor's room, he asked her to move into another until they had crossed through and gone their way. The sight of cut flowers brought him pain. All living things were included in his reverence for life.

Perhaps we would not carry reverence for life this far. Yet, I suspect that each of us is attracted to this lifestyle. At the least, we sense that this is closer to what ought to be than the callousness with which we regard much of life.

Human relationship to the animal kingdom takes several forms. The vegetarian says no killing of animals for food. This can be an ethical and/or religious position. We had a vegetarian in one of the churches we served. He used to share with us some vegetarian dishes. As we came to the bottom of the bowl, we inevitably would find a sticker which said, "Be kind to animals by not eating them."

There are others who eat meat prepared but would not kill an animal themselves. Others who eat meat also hunt animals for food. Then there are those who kill for the sake of killing, for the excitement of it, whether or not the meat is used. This is wanton killing. What is our position as Christians and Jews? Reverence for life! Yet, the Genesis word applies: humanity has dominion over all creation, and every living thing is available for food. Hunting is part of a primitive instinct. When exercised in accordance with the rules of sportsmanship with a minimum of suffering, hunting is more humane than other alternatives. I learned in Fredericksburg, Texas where I served a church, that unless humans harvest the deer, nature will do its own harvesting in a more cruel way. Hunting is wholesome recreation. When the game is used or the killing serves a purpose, hunting can be held in the context of reverence for life. Yet, perhaps there should be no killing that is not accompanied with some sense of sorrow, for life belongs to life.

Respect for Human Life

Gratitude for our life involves respect for all of life. However, this Commandment is directed mainly to human relationships. The Christian witness is that not only are our lives loved, so are the lives of others. Human life is the highest form of life that we know. "You will not kill" has profound implications for relationships between human beings. When are people killed?

Murder is one way. Murder is malicious killing motivated

by hatred, malice, or the desire for personal gain. Murder is universally recognized as wrong. The story of Cain and Abel in Genesis gives us the psychology of murder and points us to the state of separation that leads to such killing.

War is mass killing and also recognized as wrong. A social disorder or enmity between nations leads to conflict resulting in the loss of lives. At times war has seemed to be the lesser of two evils. Can it be anymore? We have come to a time when it is doubtful that war can serve as a means for deciding disputes. The cost is too great. The outlawing of war would be a great step in the humanizing of our planet.

People are killed through starvation and the lack of the basic necessities of life. It is possible to find a way to meet basic needs all across our planet. Not to do so is an offense against both God and humanity. It is incumbent upon us to find better ways of producing and distributing the basic necessities so that no one dies in dehumanized neglect.

Self-defense leads to some killing. Most of us could justify defending ourselves or others, even to the point of killing, if that were to stop an act of unlawful violence. Still, something is out of order. We are all responsible for moving society to a state where all are safe and no one is a threat to another.

Suicide perplexes us. From one perspective, our lives are not our own to take. Most of us would question this method of solving problems. Suicide denies a person, a family, and society the opportunity of healing the hurt. Yet, unusual circumstances leave us with questions. The celebrated case of the Henry Pitney Van Dusens comes to mind. They served long and well as national and international religious leaders many years ago. Elderly and in a rest home, they faced an intolerable life situation and took their own lives. Some of us wonder whether "no suicide" is an absolute.

Capital punishment has been much in the news of late. Society must be protected. No one has a right to murder and remain free. Yet, does killing someone who kills someone show that killing is wrong? One by one the nations have been abolishing capital punishment. Such a judgment on a life is playing God. Capital punishment says that all hope for redemption is gone. Have you noted that the closer we get to the direct re-sponsibility for taking the life of another, the greater the reluc-tance to see it happen?

Capital punishment? I would have to say "No!" Capital punishment makes us public murderers. Whether we pull the switch or pay to have it done, we are involved. I admit my anger and that at times I am ready emotionally for the death penalty in heinous crimes, but my mind cannot accept such an act as right and just. Keeping felons alive is a symbol of reverence for life. Killing them adds a wrong to a wrong, which hardly makes a right. Capital punishment is a pain in the soul of society and is an emotional burden on us that we do not deserve.

Abortion is another act of killing but is it murder? How fraught with emotion is this issue! We are involved in the strug-gle and must, at this point, respect differences of opinion. We all can acknowledge the mystery of the moment of conception. The union of ovum and sperm means that the 46 chromosomes are present, giving a unique genetic structure. What is the right of this unique creation? Is the embryo or fetus a human being? Is an acorn an oak tree? A human being is defined as a rational and relational creature. This is hardly the case for an embryo or fetus.

For me, human life is not mere physical existence. Forget abortion for a moment and consider the other end of life. When relational and rational capability is gone, human life has ceased, though the physical processes may continue. When the termi-nally ill arrive at this point, I am for stopping whatever activity keeps the process going. On the other hand, the fetus has future human possibilities, though not immediate capability. The aborting of the fetus is, therefore, a serious tension of life with life. Abortion simply because the child is unwanted is not for me sufficient reason. Some criteria for the unacceptability of the pregnancy must be brought to the decision. The age of the mother, rape, or something other than mere personal inconven-ience. Who makes this decision? Simply a woman and her doc-tor? This is to make the doctor a scapegoat for the judiciary, the clergy, the partners, and the parents. The medical profession should not be placed in such an untenable position. Some say that a woman has a right over her own body, but this that is conceived in her is not her own body. The fetus is already separate and unique. This means that a larger community bears some responsibility for decision-making.

In all of these issues, the primary factor is reverence for life, which involves respect for the quality of life. Jesus went past the law. He said, "You have heard that it was said to the men of old, 'You will not kill.... But I say to you that if you are angry with a brother or sister, you will be liable to judgment...."[3] More than mere physical existence is involved. A concern for the quality of life and the right relationships between human beings are primary concerns. We cannot responsibly relate to those issues on the basis of legal absolutes.

We have no simple solution to some of these problems. The need is to keep the tension, the dialogue, and the openness to one another. The key is the willingness to struggle out of reverence for life as God-given and to take seriously the Commandment:

"You will not murder."

Notes
1. Genesis 9:3
2. Luke 12:6
3. Matt. 5:22

QUESTIONS FOR REFLECTION OR DISCUSSION

1. What did "not murder" mean for the ancient Hebrew?
2. How many ways do you see killing going on?
3. How do you feel about killing animals?
4. What is the difference between killing animals and killing humans?
5. What about vegetarianism?
6. Can reverence for life be reconciled to killing humans?
7. How does life today make this Commandment more problematic?

VII
Covenants and Commitments

You will not commit adultery.

How do we keep rightly related? Whether with persons or life in general, we are in a state of flux. Life is movement from separation to reunion and from reunion to separation. Togetherness is a blessing while alienation is disturbing. The Christian perspective involves understanding that once we were no people, and now we are God's people. Christians do not always live aware of this state. Time and again we experience alienation.

Yet, we have been brought into a new covenant with God through the Jesus Christ event. This new covenant points us to reunion and return. Each service of worship we prepare again to hear this word, to understand its power, and to translate it into life. The God dimension of life has been disclosed to us in the man Jesus of Nazareth. The Christian proclamation is that God comes to us in the Jesus story, makes God's self known, and brings us to newness of life. A new covenant has been established, and our part in the covenant is loyalty and devotion. Our covenant with God in the Jesus event has implications for our other covenants. As we continue a new look at the Ten Commandments, we now consider the Seventh: "You will not commit adultery." This Commandment is a matter of covenants and commitments. Our covenant with God and such human covenants are related.

Covenants

We now take a short excursion from what most think of with the term "adultery" to consider the biblical idea of covenant. If this is not to your liking, skip to the next section. The term "covenant" implies a relationship that involves understanding, commitment, loyalty, and devotion. The covenant with God comes with a promise: I will be your God, and you will be my people. The Hebrew Scriptures speak of three major covenants: between God and Abraham (containing the promise that Abraham's descendants will be a nation and that he would be blessed in order to be a blessing to the whole world); between God and Moses, the Sinai covenant (embodying the awareness that God had set the Hebrews free and that the response of the people was to be devotion, loyalty, and obedience); the royal covenant with David (involving the conviction that from the House of David would come a new relationship not based on law but on the Spirit).

The Hebrews were aware of the covenant even in its absence. While they were in Babylonian captivity, they could not sing the Lord's song in a strange land. They wept as they remembered Zion. In Jeremiah they agitated for a return to Jerusalem. They saw alienation and return and a new relationship with their return to their homeland. This return would mean a re-established covenant which would not be forgotten. But it was.

Christian Scriptures proclaim that a new relationship has been established. We are the new people of God, and we are blessed in order to be a blessing. We have been set free for loyalty and obedience. We have been given a new spirit, the spirit evident in the person of Jesus. The covenant in Jesus has broken the barriers of natural division in the human family: racial, sexual, national. The First Peter letter, says that we are one people in this Christ event, called to sanctification by the spirit of

Jesus and for sprinkling with his blood. This is a symbolic way of saying that we are part of a new body and share in that life resurrected in the Christian community.[1]

Our covenant (or relationship) with God is eternal, abiding, everlasting, and involves our response of loyalty and obedience. The breaking of the covenant places another at the center and gives ultimate loyalty and obedience to some thing or some one other than God. This in the Bible is an adulterous relationship. The prophets were clear in their condemnation. The people went whoring after other gods, other loyalties. Adultery was forsaking the One and Eternal for a lesser god.

Like us, the Hebrews thought at times that other gods promised more. The Baalim (Phoenician and Canaanite gods) promised fertility of the soil and fruitfulness in childbearing. The gods of our day are promising pleasure, property, power, prestige and many other "blessings." But in the end all are meaningless and empty. We know the powerlessness of the gods to give life ultimate satisfaction. The covenant with God is not that God would fix anything or do anything. God would be their God; God would offer His presence and faithfulness and would be attentive to the relationship: I will be with you; I will not leave you nor forsake you. And this is what we need above all else—Presence!

Think of life today. Why do we want people in our lives? Not basically to do something for us. We want relationships to continue; we want presence. This is what God offers: God's presence, the assurance of love, being for us no matter what. This is what is revealed in the Jesus event: God as Emmanuel, with us.

Human Covenants

What does all this mean in our relative, human commitments? We give ourselves to one another. "Till death us do part," we say in the marriage vow. But death does part us. Human love is loving but being willing to let go when called upon to do so. No human relationship endures forever.

Marriage is primary among life's commitments. The Bible expresses it: "The two will become one." They do and they don't. This is a highly symbolic word. In one sense two becoming one is nonsense. Each remains a separate and unique person. The presence of two distinct and different selves is the strength of a relationship. On the other hand, the two become one physically. Flesh unites with flesh. The sexual union is a sign of oneness. They are one socially, becoming husband and wife, a couple. They are one spiritually. In giving themselves each to the other, they are, in a profound sense, joined with the self-giving love of God.

This relationship is needed, desperately needed. We need covenant and commitment. We need to be bound in order to be set free. Marriage does assault the ego, makes demands upon us, calls for disciplines, commitments, and restraints; but it is what we need. Our situation is that we are still a family-oriented society. In spite of divorce, marriage persists. Divorced people marry again. More than that, we are also expanding the concept of family to include same sex couples in committed relationships. In spite of all the controversy in both church and society, this is happening and the expansion will continue. For all its problems, marriage (by whatever name we choose to call it) continues as a union of couples committed to each other in covenant relationships.

Chief among marriage problems is the relationship each one has with others. This is where the Seventh Commandment comes into focus. "You will not commit adultery." We all think we know what this means, but do we? What is it we are not supposed to do? Where is the forsaking of the marriage covenant, and what is that covenant?

"No adultery" had a specific meaning for the ancient Hebrew. This Commandment was to protect the Hebrew male and applied only to a sexual relationship to a woman married or engaged to another. A married woman was the property of her husband. He had right to sole possession of her. Adultery was a violation of his property rights. Not only that, a man had a right to know that the children borne by his wife were his. That was the protection built into this Commandment. Otherwise, the Hebrew male was quite free.

Responsible Sexuality

We have moved past that point in history. What is responsible sexual expression? The Bible gives us no clear word for relationships between men and women. There are no laws of sexual behavior consistently spelled out. The prohibition of adultery runs all the way from the narrow definition in the Hebrew Scriptures, applied to the married woman and protecting the male, to Jesus' word that whoever has lust in his heart has already committed adultery. When is a relationship improper, or a breaking of the covenant? We are involved in gray areas and are floundering today.

All the rules are contextual, even the old ones. The Hebrew rule on adultery was contextual. The context was the property rights of the male and no birth control methods. We are in a different historical situation. Christians today are part of the changing sexual scene. Simply increasing the volume in proclaiming the old morality is not sufficient. We must speak out of today's context. Jesus was a contextual ethicist. "They said of old but I say to you ." Persons mattered to him more than rules. His yardstick was love. Laws were made for human need; and human need was prior to the law.

What, then, do we do with this Commandment? "You will not commit adultery" points to the seriousness with which we are to take our covenants and commitments. Marriage is the primary commitment. In marriage we are saying that you can count on me to be for you; I am not going to leave you for another. The breaking of the covenant is forsaking one's mate and giving loyalty and devotion elsewhere.

Promiscuous sex is, of course, part of this picture. Promiscuity has the distinction of no permanence, no structure, and no covenant. Sex is not mere pleasure, though it is pleasurable. It is not just a form of recreation though it involves leisure time. Promiscuous sex has no depths to sustain it and expresses what is not there. Sex is the sign of self-giving. With no intention to give oneself to another, sex is a lie. Sex that is simply getting what I want apart from a self-giving commitment is demeaning a depth dimension of human life. Sex needs the discipline of covenant and commitment with the full self involved. This is best expressed in the covenant of marriage.

Is the Bible a good guide for marriage? A professor of Hebrew Bible and Jewish sudies at U.C. Berkley opines that if we are going to use the Bible to define the marriage relationship, we should go all the way. What would biblical marriages look like? He suggests the following in words that I have paraphrased:

1. Marriage is the union between a man and one or more women. Many biblical marriages were polygamous even though that was decreasing in the biblical period.
2. Adultery is punishable by death. This would reduce the ranks of televangelists, Hollywood stars, and members of Congress, to mention a few groups.
3. Divorce is prohibited in the words of Jesus.
4. Marriage is preferable to sinning, according to Paul, which is not a positive view of marriage.[2]

"You will not commit adultery" has wide application in today's context. Sex can be misused in marriage as well as without. Many today have an adulterous relationship with the television set or the computer. A newspaper article sometime ago entitled "Sex and the Tube" revealed the hurt to human life that is involved in this adultery . The covenant that I will be with you, will not leave you nor forsake you, is broken again and again by television and now by the computer. This is just one example among many forms of adultery. We can have an adulterous relationship with our work, our children, or our hobbies, needlessly forsaking another.

"You will not commit adultery" involves our covenants and commitments beginning with God as the primary commitment, continuing with our spouse as the secondary commitment, and then extending to our friends and to the entire world of which we are a part. Are we, for instance, committed to the hungry of the world or to those devastated by natural disasters? To forsake them is an adulterous relationship.

Adultery is disloyalty to our deepest commitments. We are called to loyalty and obedience, being for the other and others, making our presence available where we have committed ourselves. God so commits God's self to us, and we respond in our serious commitments to one another.

"You will not commit adultery."

Notes
1. 1 Peter 1:1; 2:10
2. Ronald S. Hendel, Bible Review, October 2004

QUESTIONS FOR REFLECTION OR DISCUSSION

1. What is a covenant?
2. What is the relationship between covenants and commitments?
3. How does the covenant with God relate to our human covenants?
4. What is the ancient view of adultery?
5. Does the old concept of adultery apply differently to present life?
6. What is the relationship between adultery and sexuality?
7. Is marriage and adultery ever reconcilable?

VIII
Person and Property

You will not steal.

Ownership is both a bane and a blessing in human life. Everyone has the struggle with the proper relationship to what is owned. We cannot escape decision-making with respect to what belongs to us and what belongs to others. No wonder the Ten Commandments include two that deal specifically with ownership.

The Commandments are not the beginning nor the end of religion. As we have indicated before, they represent the gratitude response to the prior activity of God. They hold deepest meaning only when we trust in a Presence to which we are accountable. God gives a relationship and human beings respond. Unless we know the nature of the relationship, the Commandments become a burden which we either refuse to carry or obey out of fear of the consequences. To know the relationship, which involves the freeing and saving activity of God, is to see the law as a blessing—providing a witness to the right response to life by those who know the grace in which they live and move and have their being.

The last three Commandments point to a failure in the life of faith, hope and love. Without faith and hope, our relationship with our neighbor is strained. Without love, a neighbor is another object to be used for our own benefit. This leads us to the eighth Commandment: "You will not steal."

Property

Stealing is a relational sickness. The root of stealing is a lack of trust. Without trust there is no confidence in the security of one's life and little gratitude for what is owned. With such a lack, the goodness of life is not in what is but in relationship to what could be if only I had more!

Sacredness of property is now added to the sacredness of life and family. Private ownership is implied. The Hebrew Scriptures conceive of property as an extension of the self. We do become involved in what we own. Through the years I have sold several cars. I remember two because I liked them; they were fun to drive. When they were driven away by the new owners, I experienced the pain of loss. Many of you know what this means if not with a car, with some other piece of property. Collectors know this identity with what is collected. For many antique, stamp, coin or other collectors, collecting is considered as both a hobby and an investment. A problem emerges when the collector becomes so identified with the items that he or she parts with them only at great pain. I once knew a collector of antiques who rented a store but for years refused to sell anything because each item was irreplaceable.

Property is important but not all important. Property can become a barrier to the life of the spirit as we hold on desperately and as we reach out to take in more and more. But the opposite is likewise true. Lack of possessions is an almost insurmountable barrier to the life of the spirit. Property is not the end of a higher life, but it helps make it possible. The history of humanity is the story of the struggle with the elements. When on the verge of starvation with no property, a hand-to-mouth existence, human beings have had little culture. Leisure time is needed to develop the life of the spirit, and leisure comes with property.

The accumulation of wealth means so much that we value

it highly. On the other hand, great accumulation is question-able, not because property is evil but because it is good and ought to be part of the lives of more people; and accumulation is often at the expense of others. The psalmist was right: "... if riches increase, set not your heart on them."[1] Luther wrote somewhere: "Do not be anxious about your life" does not mean not working. A chicken won't fly into your mouth. By all means work for wealth, but keep free from the worrying and greedy anxiety that thinks that there will never be enough.

Stealing

Consider now the Commandment more intensely: "You will not steal." If this had said you will not steal money, this would not bother me so much; but without the object this Commandment exposes much more of life.

Originally this Commandment prohibited kidnapping, the stealing of a person. Later it came to mean much more than that. Luther applied this Commandment to anything that takes away from or hinders a neighbor in the use of his possessions or works against his increasing them. Transgressors included in Luther's list are those who practice thievery, robbery, or usury; who use false weights and measures; who receive bequests and income dishonestly; who withhold wages earned; who do not protect another against loss; who do not warn another against loss; who place an obstacle in the way of his neighbor's profit and begrudge his gain. Luther goes on to say that the proper work to guard against any form of stealing is benevolence: good will toward others based on love of one's own life and love of others. This means the refusal to gain for yourself at the other's expense. How hard it is to see ourselves guilty, to notice our lust for the possessions or prestige of another, or to see our focus on what we can do to further our own ends at the expense of an-other.

Job cried, "If ... my mouth has kissed my hand; ... I should have been false to God above."[2] The offense is the pride and sat-isfaction in gaining something we have not earned and praising our sleight of hand in the process. Years ago I noticed a cover on the *Saturday Evening Post* by Norman Rockwell. The scene was a meat counter. On the scales was a slab of meat. On one side the butcher was looking up at the reading, but his finger was pushing down gently on the scales to increase the weight. On the other side of the machine was a gray-haired, saintly-looking woman whose finger was gently pushing up on the scales. The humor is there but also the tragedy. Each was trying to gain an advantage over the other.

Our culture is suffering from lack of moral consciousness. In business, loyalty is valued more than conscience. Norman Cousins, one of the most respected writers of the last century, once mentioned that those who spill the beans and blow the whistle on fraudulent acts are penalized. A defect in our society exists when those who call attention to wrong-doing are ostracized. We have seen this time and again in recent days. No wonder some are disillusioned by virtues they once believed in.

Stealing goes on in all kinds of ways. A West Point cheating scandal years ago was much in the news that illustrated cheating as a form of stealing. How did all this happen? Listen to this fabrication: Johnny at six years old was riding with his father when a policeman stopped them for speeding. Along with the driver's license, Johnny's father gave the officer a ten-dollar bill who promptly gave him a warning and let him go on his way. Johnny looked questioningly, and his father said, "Don't worry about it; everybody does it." At eight years of age, Johnny's aunt had taken him to a grocery store. On the way to the car after the purchases, she mentioned happily that the clerk had given her change for a ten dollar bill when she had only given her a five. Johnny looked surprised, so she responded, "Don't worry about it; everybody does it." When he was ten, Johnny's uncle had taken him to an event marked "Sold out." His uncle walked up to an attendant and slipped him a bill, and they were furtively let in. The uncle said to Johnny, "Don't worry about it; everybody does it." At age 12 Johnny broke his glasses. His mother told him that they would report it to the insurance company as having been lost and they would be replaced. "Don't worry about it; everybody does it." When Johnny was 15 his football coach taught him how to get hold of an opponent's jersey so as not to be seen by the referee. "Don't worry about it; everybody does it." At 19 he was at West Point. An upper-classman told him that he had a copy of an examination that Johnny could have for ten dollars. Johnny was caught and sent home in disgrace. His parents said, "How could you do this to us?" And his aunt and uncle were shocked. The one thing this adult world cannot stand is a kid who cheats.[3]

Applications and Implications

This Commandment has many applications. Consider another issue: state lotteries. At one time the numbers game was denounced by states as a racket and fraud. Most were convinced that it was immoral to take money from people when they have less than one chance in a million of getting anything for their funds. Now a number of states have legalized lotteries. Are the odds any better now that state governments are behind them?

What about the ethical use of money? In purchasing we trade value for value. In investing we offer time with our funds and expect some gain. In speculation (which should be practiced by only those who can afford to lose) we risk our money in a venture that could produce substantial returns but might also lose our investment. Gambling (lottery, for instance) has a fraction of one percent probability of winning anything. Stealing varies from gambling by a fraction of a percent. Of course gambling is with the consent of the gambler and stealing is without that consent, but the difference otherwise is negligible.

What does it mean when the state, which is dedicated to "preserving the general welfare," becomes involved in advertising to entice people to gamble? Often the people who are least able to afford the risk are tempted to gamble to augment their limited funds. Thus the state preys upon those very people whose general welfare should be the state's concern.

The young are not oblivious of the fact that many portions of society take unfortunate advantage of others. Insider trading, the falsification of bills, cheating by repair people, doctors profiteering from Medicare and Medicaid, and a variety of "professionals" who make every effort to get what the market will bear are examples of more than cheating. These all are forms of stealing.

Stealing in any of its varied forms is a failure of love. When we look closely, we can see how we are tempted. But when we are aware of that Presence that is the source of unbounded love, gratitude calls from us the loving response to our neighbor. We can love, and not take unfair advantage of the other, because God first loved us.

Notes
1. Psalm 62:10
2. Job 31:27
3. From notes taken on "Cheaters Unlimited," Saturday Review of Literature, 10/16/76

QUESTIONS FOR REFLECTION OR DISCUSSION

1. What is the tension about ownership?
2. What is the sickness involved in stealing?
3. How can property become a barrier in relationships?
4. How do you feel about the accumulation of much wealth?
5. Can stealing ever be justified?
6. Can you relate stealing and cheating?
7. What is the difference between stealing and gambling?

IX

The Unruly Tongue

You will not bear false witness against your neighbor.

How many see Christianity as a restriction of life: don't do this, don't do that, don't do something else! Such an attitude is based on a wrong view of the law. The law can be a weight holding us down or it can serve as wings keeping us going in the right direction. Our response depends on whether we see laws as legalistic impositions or as guides. The psalmist loved the law: "O how I love Your law! It is my meditation all the day. Your commandment makes me wiser than my enemies, for it is ever with me."[1]

We have lost such an appreciation for the law. Can such be recovered? We have been examining the Ten Commandments through the Good News of the Christian Gospel. Jesus placed the ten (five focused on the love of God and five on the love of neighbor) into two: "You will love the Lord your God with all your heart, and with all your soul, and with all your mind...." And a second is like it, "You will love your neighbor as yourself."[2]

The love of God and neighbor is possible because of a prior love. We love because He first loved us. The love of God and neighbor is a reflection of the love by which we are loved. Yet, how many hate their lives and live with constant complaining and chronic dissatisfaction! This often leads to the attempt to lift self up by putting other people down. How unnecessary! All things are ours: the past, the present, the future; life, creation, family, friends, the world. The Commandments serve as guides, pointing us to the life of love. The Commandments, too, are ours, not as a burden, but a blessing.

So it is with the next one in our series: "You will not bear false witness against your neighbor." The Good News is that we do not have to do so.. We gain no benefit. We are already made right by the accepting love of God disclosed to us in the Jesus Christ event.

This Commandment's Meaning

What is this Commandment all about? The ancient Hebrew was admonished not to testify as a lying witness. In the court of elders which met at the city gates, he was to be a true witness. No one should for any purpose testify falsely. The Hebrew Scriptures were so insistent on justice that no one was to be put to death on the testimony of one witness alone. The ancient code of the Babylonian king, Hammurabi (about 2,000 BCE and pre-dating the Hebrew Scriptures), says that a false witness will have done to him what was to be done to the accused. We continue to hold in utter seriousness the testimony in a court of law. Perjury at the expense of others is a crime.

Later interpretation of this Commandment included every false statement, in court and out, in which the neighbor's name and reputation were at stake. Slander, defamation of character, and idle gossip are all involved. These are bad news and an indication of the non-acceptance of a relationship to God.

Gossip is stealing another's reputation. Gossip is carnivorous; it consumes people. As Walter Wangerin, Jr. describes it someplace: "Gossip is verbal slaughter." This is the sin of slander. One whose own life is missing joy and satisfaction demeans another's life in an effort at self-elevation. Or, the opposite is also true: when self-righteousness increases, so does gossip. To the misuse of hand and eye in the Commandments against stealing and coveting (next chapter) is now added the tongue.

An unruly tongue to seek some advantage over another is a rejection of the Good News that God is for us. Shakespeare was concerned about the misuse of the tongue when he had Iago say in Othello:

> *Good name in man and woman, dear my Lord,*
> *Is the immediate jewel of their souls;*
> *Who steals my purse steals trash; 'tis*
>   *something, nothing;*
> *'Twas mine, 'tis his, and has been slave*
>   *to thousands;*
> *But he that filches from me my good name*
> *Robs me of that Which not enriches him,*
> *And makes me poor indeed.*

Martin Luther saw the transgressors of this Commandment as:

> *He who conceals or suppresses the truth in court.*
> *He who lies or deceives to another's hurt.*
> *All hurtful flatterers, whisperers, double dealers.*
> *He who speaks evil of neighbors, possessions,*
>   *life, words, and works, and defames them.*
> *He who gives place to slanderers, helps them on*
>   *and does not resist them.*
> *He who does not use his tongue to defend his*
>   *neighbor's good name.*
> *He who conceals or does not defend the truth.*

To fulfill this Commandment, says Luther, is to have a peaceful, wholesome tongue that injures no one and profits all. This was Peter in the novel *Exit 36* by Robert Ferrar Capon. In the words of the author, "... he would drop their priceless trash (gossip) into the incinerator of his silence ... he had ... a quiet, deep conviction that junk should not be allowed to spoil anybody's party."[3]

Lying

Let us go further. This Commandment points us to the whole subject of lying. How much of life is corrupted because of untruth! We try to protect ourselves from some criticism or some mistake and become enmeshed with falsehoods. We try to justify ourselves, but we are already justified in the accepting love of God. In the words of the psalmist quoted in I Peter:

> *Those who desire life*
> *and desire to see good days,*
> *let them keep their tongues from evil*
> *and their lips from speaking deceit;*
> *let them turn away from evil and do good;*
> *let them seek peace and pursue it.*[4]

Our world is filled with lies! Every day on our television sets we hear statements which we know are not so. The right toothpaste does not get the boyfriend back. The right lotion cannot make you lovable. One shampoo does not make you more attractive than all the others. And in political speeches we hear innuendoes and outright falsities to undermine the character and integrity of one's opponent. We hear untruth constantly and come to accept a life in which the truth is often hidden.

Lying is wrong because it preys upon the neighbor. Lying is non-loving when it leads others to form judgments not in accord with the facts. Lying takes the instrument of knowledge, uses it for falsehood, and makes confusion. This has been so for a long time and among God's special people! In the Jacob-Esau stories, Jacob conspires with his mother to deceive Isaac. Jacob, the favorite son of Rebekah, dresses like Esau in order that blind Isaac will give him the blessing. The lies build up. "I am Esau!" But he wasn't. He felt like Esau with the skin of an animal on his arms; he smelled like Esau; but he was not Esau. The deception brought enmity between the brothers and corrupted Jacob. He suffered the consequences.[5] God's people are not immune from lying, but neither are they spared the suffering.

Truth-telling has never been an endearing virtue. We lie thinking that some good will come to us from it. We plan to lift up ourselves in deceiving another. However, whatever momentary elevation of self is experienced is soon lost in self-disgust at our mendacity.

Truth-telling in Love

Yet, this does not conclude the matter. The opposite of lying is truth-telling. The truth is what corresponds with reality. The great discipline of life is to know what is real and true. The greatest foe of lying is knowledge and understanding that comes from community. Even the most brilliant learn little by themselves. We need each other. Knowledge comes with language, a product of community; and truth is language and facts held together.

But truth is not for truth's sake, but for people's sake. In the Apostle Paul's words, we are called to speak the truth in love. What is the loving thing? To let someone get away with wrongdoing is not love. Actions that are destructive to society must be reported. This is not slander but truth-telling and conforming to reality. Someone gets hurt, but the hurt is for his or her own good and the protection of society.

To tell the truth in love keeps us from the brutal frankness that serves no purpose but truth itself. Truth-telling that is hurtful, degrading, or demeaning is not in love. Calling attention to another's physical weaknesses or deformities is not helpful or loving truth-telling.

Keeping the truth in order to give a person time to be able to receive it is sensible and loving. We do not need to give all the facts to one just out of surgery. Yet, I do not believe that it is to another's advantage to continue to believe something not true. The truth in love is sharing reality without destroying all the hope in the process.

By truthfulness we win the confidence and goodwill of others. The truth told in love is caring as much about our neighbor's needs as our own. Telling such truth is not always easy, but it is the loving and caring response that allows another to deal with reality.

Faith and confidence give us the freedom from the lying that separates us from the truth. "Stand by the truth," said Luther, "though it costs us life or cloak; though it is against pope or king." "Speak the truth in love," says Paul, "for he who loves can do no ill to the neighbor."

This Commandment together with the others forms the charter of freedom which God has given us out of history: not as a burden, but a gift; not as weight, but wings; not to restrict life, but to enlarge the possibilities for the thankful and loving response to God's presence and activity. In this perspective we, too, can say: :O how I love Your law!"

"You will not bear false witness against your neighbor."

Notes
1. Psalm 19:27-28
2. Matthew 22: 27, 29
3. *Exit 36*, Robert Ferrar Kapon, The Seabury Press, N.Y., 1975, pg. 88.
4. 1 Peter 3:10 -11
5. Genesis 27 ff.

QUESTIONS FOR REFLECTION OR DISCUSSION

1. How is truth-telling related to justice?
2. What is gossip?
3. How is gossip related to truth-telling?
4. When are we most tempted to lie?
5. Should we always tell the truth?
6. How are lying and love related?

X
Inordinate Desire

You will not covet … anything that belongs to your neighbor.

The subject of this chapter is coveting or envying. If there is a universal sin among the last five Commandments, coveting is it. Almost everyone envies or covets a good portion of the time, but doing so never feels good. (I am going to use envy and covet synonymously.) Here is the one sin of injustice without a payoff. The others seem to produce some temporary benefit for the self. Envy, on the other hand, is non-productive and begins and ends with self torment. Angus Wilson, writing about the Seven Deadly Sins, has written: "Envy wears an uglier face than Lust's bloodshot eyes, Gluttony's paunch, and Avarice's thin lips. Envy is the hardest sin to confess. Yet if we did, we would be on our knees longer."

What Is It To Covet?

In simplest terms, to covet is the bitter, resentful feeling toward one who is superior to us in possessions, talents or graces. On a continuum scale in which covet is one pole, the other would be our wants. It is all right to have wants. We want to accomplish. We want to have. We want to do. Our wants move to

71

covet on the scale when we see in others what we want, resent what we see, and wish that we had what they have.

Envying or coveting is a combination of desire and resentment. It works against us. Envy does not alert us, motivate us, liberate us or improve us. Milton said that envy is the Devil's own emotion. In *Paradise Lost*, Satan sees Adam and Eve in love. He envies and plots their downfall.

To covet is a sin in personal relationships. It involves an attitude toward another. On my side I see something that I must have, be or accomplish; but you are preventing me, or reminding me by your success that I don't have what I want so desperately.

Envy begins naturally with children. A child wanting exclusive possession of one parent will envy the other parent's or a sibling's closeness. Children sense that they are in a competition for love. Envy will include also the toys, pets, clothing or food of some other. Who has not heard: "He has a bigger piece than I have!"

In adolescence, to covet is to want another's athletic prowess, scholastic achievement or good looks. When unhappy a youth can envy the happiness of another. The euphoria of another can be distressing and lead to resentment.

Envy can become a lifestyle in adults in relationship to property, position, prestige or prominence in the community. Envy is different from avarice or greed which is a holding on and wanting more of what one already has. The envious person regrets what is the neighbor's and wants it. John of Damascus wrote that envy is sorrow for another's good and delight in another's downfall.

The Bible has many illustrations of coveting. In the competition of those with a close relationship, we need only remind ourselves of Cain and Abel, Jacob and Esau, Joseph and his brothers, and the elder son and the prodigal in Jesus' parable. In addition, the Hebrew Scripture has a story about Saul and David that is a graphic illustration of the effects of envy.

David is a military leader in Saul's army. He was so successful that the populace hailed him as a hero. It was galling for Saul to hear them singing:

"Saul has slain his thousands, and David his ten thousands." Saul's envy of David grew. He became more insecure. Finally he defeats himself. Saul's envy turns to fear and then to hate. He strikes out blindly and tries to kill David, to pin him against the wall with a javelin. In the story the more desperate Saul gets the more popular David becomes. It takes great maturity to watch someone younger and more able to begin to move up and threaten one's position.[1]

A fascinating biblical phrase is in the story: "Saul eyed David." The Latin word "invidia" means to look maliciously upon. To covet is a sin of the eyes. To covet or to envy causes us to narrow the openings and to tighten the eyelids. Try it and you will discover that in just the effort to squint, envy is close at hand. The poet Dante has those who envied in Purgatory. In a terrible image, he has the eyes of the covetous closed by the drawing of threads of iron wire through the lids. Envious eyes could not bear to look upon the joy of others and are doomed to be closed, no longer to see goodness or to be able to look into the eyes of others. Dante shudders over the curse as he hears Guido of Duca wail:

> Envy so parch'd my blood, that had I seen
> A fellow made joyous, thou hadst mark'd
> A livid paleness overspread my cheek.

The eyes of those who covet find nothing to love in this world. If someone gains, I must be losing. Someone else's good is my own deprivation.

In the Gospel of Mark Jewish leaders bring Jesus to Pilate. Pilate "perceived that it was out of envy that the chief priest delivered him up." Jesus was a young upstart from Galilee. His preaching and teaching attracted many. He spoke as one having authority in himself and not as their authority which was the law. No wonder they were envious.

Envy's Steps

Envy has a definite progression. It moves from the feeling

of deprivation to the awareness that others have what I do not. A feeling of impotence follows which adds a resentful quality to envy. Then envy's move is from comparison to competition. I don't have because they have.

One author I read some time ago illustrates envy out of personal experience. He and another professor ate lunch together each week at a roadside cafe. They were in the habit of ordering the same thing: a meatloaf sandwich on a poppyseed bun with a pickle and a drink. One week the author noticed that his colleague was not listening to him while the cook was preparing the sandwich. Week after week he noticed this same procedure and became convinced that his colleague was obsessed with what he saw to be an injustice. He was given the smaller piece of meatloaf each time, or so he thought. One week the author upon receiving his plate switched it with his friend's, who promptly exclaimed, "Why did you do that?" To which the author responded, "She made a mistake and gave you the larger piece this week." They had a good laugh over the subtle bit of comparing into which each of us is trapped at times.

Envy often creeps in unawares. We are not always sure why we are dejected. An unemployed actress I read about was in a depressed state and was receiving counseling. In the midst of this process, she did receive a part in a play to her great joy. Finally she was working and satisfied with herself and her possibilities. The next day she picked up a paper and read about a friend of hers, who also had been out of work, who received an important part in a film. The actress immediately was plunged into a state of depression. She went back to the counselor who helped her to see what was going on. She finally admitted: "In order for me to be happy, it is not enough that I succeed. My friends have to fail." The recognition of that trap of envy helped her to emerge from her depression. To covet or envy is both dissatisfaction with oneself and resentment toward some other.

Destructive Effects of Coveting

The effects of coveting can be spelled out in more detail. To covet separates us from ourselves. The lack of self-acceptance and the accompanying self-loathing dominate us. Envy demands that we not be what we are. What are we? Each of us is a body with tendencies, energy levels, IQs varied gifts and graces all coming from the Mystery of life's origins. We are life's (God's) gift to ourselves. We have great differences, but these differences enrich life. For example, some have more energy than others. The get-up-and-go energy drive of some is envied by others. Our society has a way of rewarding the high drivers. Lower energy people can be consumed by envy. Yet, lower energy people are just as valuable. They are more thoughtful and contemplative in nature and are needed just as much in society as the high energy people. Envy causes us to be blind to our own qualities and oblivious to the gifts that we have to offer.

Envy converts a person into a grievance collector. Every turn is the wrong one. My lane is the slowest. This seat is the worst. The receptionist in the restaurant is trying to seat me in a less desirable place. I am being mistreated. The envious are forever guarding themselves against potential slights. They have a love for fault finding.

Envy separates us from others. The life of resentment leaves us rather alone. In the judgment of those who envy, others are in the major leagues with jobs, property, mate, children, whatever; while they themselves are in the minors with drudgery, bad news, trouble and other forms of deprivation. Others are seen in adversarial terms in the drive to become the best lawyer, teacher, scientist, salesperson or something else. We are constantly reminded of some other's superior nature. Others appear larger than life with no needs. The wound of envy is absence of healthy relationships. Others are constant threats and reminders of our failures.

Coveting reduces ambition to meanness and pettiness. We desire not so much to do well as that others do worse. This leads to hardness of heart and bitterness of spirit, hardly the qualities that endear us to others. We become sowers of strife between colleagues, neighbors and friends. Distrust of others dominates the coveting personality and the murmurings against others never seem to stop. One of the most unfortunate aspects of envy is back-biting, the chipping away at the reputation of others. A fault is taken and made an obsession. We want to cancel the other out or, at the very least, to bring them down from their high position to our level. The envious people find their weapons: verbal darts and poisoned barbs that penetrate and destroy the other.

Envy also separates us from God. The prayer life of those who envy is more like begging for some state evident in others. Envy is poisonous in wanting God to bless us to be like others. This is intercession in reverse—lack of concern for others and more focus on ourselves. The prayer of gratitude is strangely absent. Envy can find nothing for which to be grateful. Life is unfair.

No one has to be envious. The cure or the correction is at hand. Goethe, the German poet, said: "Against another's great merits, there is no remedy but love." When love enters as a ruling passion in one's life, envying or coveting slips away. How does this come about? Christians proclaim that the event we call Jesus Christ breaks the power of sin. He, who was of the house and lineage of David, still comes to the envious Sauls of the world. He had and has nothing that makes him a threat. Think of it. He was called Son of God, Messiah, Prophet, Teacher, Healer, King of Kings, Heavenly Priest; but he dies on a cross. He is the king with no subject, the teacher with no pupils, the priest who has no sacrifice to make other than himself. He is divested of all worldly status. He has nothing except one thing, his love. He loved and forgave. He still reaches out to unite us to himself and not with any worldly accomplishment, position, or success.

That is the Gospel word in the Christian story, and it still has the power to unite us in love. In the world's eye we are always separated: one has a good grade, another does not. One receives a promotion, the other doesn't. One gets tenure, the other is passed by. One has health, the other becomes ill. One knows wealth, the other has economic strain. But in God's love revealed in the Christ event, we are all one. He does not so divide us into the haves and the have nots, the brilliant and the stupid, the beautiful and the homely, the busy and the lonely. In this one we call Christ, the very activity of God, there is no distinction. We are one in the love of God. It is not necessary to experience every joy. We receive our own lives as loved and accepted in spite of our hurts; and we recognize that whatever other people have, they also hurt.

The legacy of Martin Luther King, Jr. is in this very truth. He was able to identify with the white community. He discovered that American whites were deprived, that discrimination was hurting them as well as the blacks. His non-violent approach to change was filled with compassion for the oppressor. He was rich in God and led many into a like perspective, praying for release for the whites. On the other hand some who have suffered discrimination have been gripped by envy. Angry outbursts that often led to violence gave evidence that they were not able so to identify. Envy led inevitably to malice, then hatred and into violence. Anger, though perhaps justified, was non-productive.

The cure for envy and covetousness is the strange union between the love of God and the love for humanity. Christianity is not always what it was meant to be. Two errors have prevailed down through the centuries. The first is seeing Christianity as only the vertical dimension of God's relationship to the individual. This has been with us a long time. This is a pious view of the Christian faith. I don't need the Christian community. My relationship with God is personal. He is there with me, and I can pull God out anytime I have a need. This is cheap grace with no Christ-like compassion and concern for others. How can we love God whom we have not seen if we do not love our neighbor who we do see?

The other error is seeing Christianity on strictly the horizontal plane: my relationship to the neighbor. This newer error is found in simple humanism. Religion is my relationship to my brothers and sisters. I am to love others and do good in this world. The problem is this leads either to despair when my good does not seem to accomplish much or to pride as I pile up my merits. But where in this point of view is the perspective that enables me to love and care for the enemy, for those who would nail me to a cross? As Jesus said: "For if you love those who love you, what reward have you?"

It is time to unite the two, the vertical and the horizontal. The cross does this and serves as the appropriate symbol for the union between God and humanity. The Church at its best has always held the vertical and horizontal dimensions together. This is done in the proclamation of the gospel, in the fellowship of the Church and in the services that the Church renders to the world. God unites us with others. His love works to overcome the separation that envy and covetousness cause. God's love through us to others is part of that faith that overcomes the world.

"You will not covet ... anything that belongs to your neighbor."

Note

1. 1 Samuel 18

Questions for Reflection or Discussion

1. What is the relationship between coveting and envying?
2. Can one envy without coveting?
3. What does envying do to human relationships?
4. How does envying relate to a bodily function? (Dante)
5. What is the corrective to coveting or envying?

Appendix A
The Ten Commandments

Exodus

20 And God spoke all these words:

2 I am the Lord your God, who brought you out of the land of Egypt, out of the house of slavery.

3 You will have no other gods before me,

4 You will not make for yourself an idol, whether in the form of anything that is in heaven above, or that is on the earth beneath, or that is in the water under the earth. 5 you will not bow down to them or worship them; for I the Lord your God am a jealous God, punishing children for the iniquity of parents, to the third and the fourth generation of those who reject me,

6 but showing steadfast love to the thousandth generation of those who love me and keep my commandments.

7You will not make wrongful use of the name of the Lord your God; for the Lord will not acquit anyone who misuses his name.

8 Remember the sabbath day, and keep it holy. 9 Six days you will labor, and do all your work; 10 but the seventh day is a sabbath to the Lord your God; you will not do any work—you, your son, or your daughter, your male or your female slave, your livestock, or the alien resident in your towns. 11For in six days the Lord made heaven and earth, the sea, and all that is in them, but rested the seventh day; therefore the Lord blessed the sabbath day and consecrated it.

12 Honor your father and your mother, that your days may be long in the land that the Lord your God is giving you.

13 You will not murder.

14 You will not commit adultery.

15 You will not steal.

16 You will not bear false witness against your neighbor.

17 You will not covet your neighbor's house; you will not covet your neighbor's wife, or male or female slave, or ox, or donkey, or anything that belongs to your neighbor.

Deuteronomy

5 6 I am the Lord your God, who brought you out of the land of Egypt, out of the house of slavery.

7 You will have no other gods before me.

8 You will not make for yourself an idol whether in the form of anything that is in heaven above, or that is on the earth beneath, or that is in the water under the earth; 9 You will not bow down to them or worship them; for I the Lord your God am a jealous God, punishing children for the iniquity of parents to the third and fourth generation of those who reject me, 10 but showing steadfast love to the thousandth generation of those who love me and keep my commandments.

11 You will not make wrongful use of the name of the Lord your God; for the Lord will not acquit anyone who misuses his name.

12 Observe the sabbath day and keep it holy, as the Lord your God commanded you. 13 Six days you will labor, and do all your work; 14 but the seventh day is a sabbath to the Lord your God; you will not do any work—you, or your son, or your daughter, or your male or female slave, or your ox, or your donkey, or any of your livestock, or the resident alien in your towns, so that your male and female slave may rest as well as you. 15 Remember that you were a slave in the land of Egypt, and the Lord our God brought you out from there with a mighty hand and an outstretched arm; therefore the Lord your God commanded you to keep the sabbath day.

16 Honor your father and your mother, as the Lord your God commanded you; so that your days may be long, and that it may go well with you, in the land that the Lord your God is giving you.

17 You will not murder.

18 Neither will you commit adultery.

19 Neither will you steal.

20 Neither will you bear false witness against your neighbor.

21 Neither will you covet your neighbor's wife; and you will not desire your neighbor's house, or field, or his male or female slave, ox, or donkey, or anything that belongs to your neighbor.

Appendix B
The Ten Commandments
An Opinion Scale★

What Are They?

1. Absolute laws given by God to be obeyed.

2. A moral code given by God to the ancient Hebrews to be transmitted to succeeding generations for the benefit of all humanity.

3. God-given laws which offer us the key to a way of life that finds favor with God.

4. Laws emerging from the life of God-sensitive Hebrews, in their attempt to order their lives, and offering insights for us today.

5. Historically relative laws which must be interpreted in every age in the light of changing circumstances.

6. Laws given by God for the Hebrew people having historical interest but now replaced by the teachings of Jesus.

7. Old laws once helpful but no longer relevant for contemporary life.

Instructions:

a. Do not put your name on the paper.

b. Circle the number of that opinion that comes closest to your own. Circle one only!

c. Do not fold the paper but turn upside down and pass around to the teacher.

d. Post results on marker board to indicate where the class is.

★ For duplication and use in class session

Addenda
Essays on the Commandments

*(Three biblical essays related to the Commandments,
the Law, human freedom, and unmerited love)*

I
THE NEW LOOK

Where is the authority for the Christian life? Some say it is
in the Church and Church traditions. All matters of faith and
morals depend upon the Church's teaching. But in matters of
tradition one generation's truth is another generation's trap.
This has been the case with divorce, birth control, and other
personal behavior. Others say that the authority rests in the
Bible, so that it is sufficient to ask of every moral or spiritual
question, "What does the Bible say?" But the Bible suffers from
varieties of interpretations, and many subjects of twentieth century concern are missing from its pages. Still others hold that
authority is vested in the Spirit, that God gives the Holy Spirit
to those who submit to God in faith. But what is the Spirit, and
where is it?

Where is our authority, and how do we find it? Must we remain in darkness? Christians celebrate the coming of the light:
Jesus whom we call Christ. (See note following.) There was
light before Jesus. The psalmist called the Bible, which was for
him the law, a light: "Your word is a lamp to my feet and a light
to my path." (Ps. 119:105) The Gospel of John calls Jesus the
light of the world. This is a light which gives us a fresh look at
the Bible and helps us to see the law and especially the Ten
Commandments anew.

Note: The term "Christ" is the Greek translation of the Hebrew "Messiah." This one was supposed to be the activity of God bringing back the David monarchy. Christians adopted the term to refer to the redemptive activity of God they discovered in Jesus. They gave Jesus this title though he was not the one the Hebrews expected.

The New Covenant

Paul as a faithful Jew struggled with the old and the new. Speaking to Christians, he said, "God ... has made us competent to be ministers of a new covenant, not of letter but of spirit; for the letter kills, but the Spirit gives life." (2 Cor. 3:6) All Christians are ministers, not a few chosen out of the Church. All of us are called to be ministers of the covenant. We are confused by this word "covenant." The Latin translation of the Scriptures translated "covenant " by "testamentum" from which we get Old Testament and New Testament. More accurately, this is the Old Covenant and the New Covenant.. We could also use the old agreement and new agreeement, or the old relationship and the new. However, in order not to infer that the Hebrew understanding is out of date (which it isn't), I prefer referring to Scriptures as Hebrew and Christian.

Paul infers that we are letters from Christ. In ancient civilizations letters were on stone. The Ten Commandments, tradition tells us, were written on stone tablets. This story had a splendor and glory about it; but in the new relationship in Christ, the splendor is so much greater! The glory of the ancient story is far surpassed by the glory of the new. How many of us can illustrate this from the story of our love life. As youth we were attracted by a pretty or a handsome face. We knew the excitement of the love attraction. Our behavior changed in relationship to this person. But later in life, when a deeper relationship became possible with another, and a whole person was loved, body, mind, and spirit, the splendor far exceeded the splendor of that earlier infatuation.

Paul saw the new relationship in Christ far exceeding the

relationship to the law. In fact, he said that the written code kills but this new relationship gives life. The old has been caught up in the new; we are celebraters of a New Covenant. A new light has come into the world, giving us a new look at ourselves and others. The new look is celebrated in the service of Holy Communion as well as in every service of worship.

The Old Covenant

To see what this really means, look again at the Old Covenant, the law, the religion of the book. Hebrew Scripture has 613 regulations, the primary being, variously called, the Ten Words, the Decalogue, or the Ten Commandments. Roman law had 2,414 canons, which shows how far a legal code can go to try to govern life. But in case you think that is excessive, I have been told that the effort to codify the Texas laws and regulations involves over 18,000 pages.

The Ten Commandments, in particular, speak to the pressure points of life, the areas of greatest conflict, tension, and frustration: money, sex, power, ambition, politics, justice. The present form had a long, historical development. The areas treated were of extreme importance for the life of a community. In these Commandments, we are dealing with a magnificent statement of moral and ethical law. The glory of the Ten Commandments is found in their stark simplicity and objectivity. The Ten are comprehensive, offering a remarkable breadth which sets them apart from other laws.

The Commandments are set in the context of creation itself, the way life is. The Commandments chart the outer limits of the covenant and give a positive context for life. Israel was promised a great future if she would obey and suffering if she did not. The law code represents a higher form of religion than had been known. The law implies that the world is based on moral order. The law is a restraining force to a people who were tempted to idolatry and injustice. The law is also an ideal. The Hebrew grew to love the law. "Oh, how I love your law!" cried the psalmist. (Ps. 119:97) A law like this or any law gives us security. We know what we have to do: this and no less, which can be irksome; or, this and no more, which can be very congenial.

But no law can envisage all possibilities, take into account all cases or close all gaps. On the surface the law seems easy as a guide to one's life. We see clear limits, and we know when we have done our duty. If I achieve, I can expect a reward. The whole system of debits and credits is part of the law, giving us hope that at some final accounting the scales will be balanced in our favor.

Yet both Hebrew and Christian Scriptures give testimony that obedience is beyond human possibility. Jeremiah looked ahead to a new law, written not on tablets but on the human heart. Paul loved the law but came to see its insufficiency. The law is not the full expression of God's will. The written code is not enough and, in fact, is deadly in its effect.

The law expresses a duty but gives no power to perform the duty. Legal religion gives external authority but no inner motivation. The Old Covenant is still with us. If not the Ten Commandments, the Sermon on the Mount, or some other body of teaching directs us. Yet, the written code kills no matter its origin.

We face today the dangers of a book religion. Doing God's will has too easily been identified with obeying some law, but it is not so simple. The law leads to legalism. We must keep the law, and God is our judge. But, finally, we are all found wanting. The end of legalism is death, so Paul says. The Law kills hope, for it cannot be kept; and frustration and despair are the result. Legalism kills life, for it earns us only condemnation. It kills strength, for it tells us what to do and offers us no help in doing it. It is no wonder that Jesus gave the death blow to legalism in religion. No one earns his or her status with God. Jesus is reported to have said, "... when you have done all that you were ordered to do, say, 'We are worthless slaves; we have done only what we ought to have done!'" (Luke 17:10) Our relationship to God is not established by a code of law. We need a new relationship. And that is just what is given to us.

Spirit, Love, and Freedom

The New Covenant in the Jesus Christ event is a covenant in the Spirit. We submit not to the law but to the presence of God. Jesus is not a legislator. He summons the individual to obedience to God, to a Presence, to love; and he identifies where this is: "Whoever has seen me has seen the Father." (John 14:9) We are called to relate as the God revealed in Jesus relates, in compassion and justice. What this means in specifics is left to us to work out.

The Sermon on the Mount is not a more strict law but words pointing to the gift of life and the grace of God. Everyone is called into relationship, and everyone has salvation offered without achievement. The Ten Commandments are preserved on a higher plane. The way of Christ is not a way of law but a way of doing God's will in each particular case to the advantage of others. The Christian distinction is not individual precepts or prohibitions but faith in the One revealed in Jesus. Jesus is a person and not a principle.

The command of love is not a new law, but the essence of law, the meaning of law. The New Covenant is an invitation of open access to God who is love involved in the struggles of life. As Matthew says in the crucifixion narrative, "... the curtain of the temple was torn in two, from top to bottom." (Matt. 27:51) This is to say that the crucifixion reveals One who is not hidden but revealed. The new relationship to God in Jesus is forgiveness, love, and acceptance producing repentance, surrender, and openness to the new.

We see this contrast in the story of the Prodigal Son. The Prodigal, who wasted his life in profligate living, was a man aware of the Law. He saw himself as disobedient. He went back expecting to be one of the hired servants submissive to the father. The elder brother was also focused on the Law. He felt that his brother did not deserve to be well-treated by the father. He could not tolerate the father's expressions of love to his wayward son. The son needed to be penalized and punished for his disobedience! But the father was in a new relationship. He greeted the Prodigal, put his arms around him, and took him back. He wanted only the son's trust and love. In gratitude for the son's return, the father planned a celebration. (Luke 15:11ff)

The New Covenant or new relationship is such a radical responsiveness and freedom. Some of you may paint. True art is not painting by the numbers, which is slavish obedience to the law. All number ones are to be painted yellow; number twos brown; number threes green. This is a mechanical process! We may conclude with a picture; and if you are not an artist, this may be better than nothing; but it is hardly art. True art comes out of love, excitement, and creativity. Real art is free response to the goodness of creation and confidence in one's ability to deal with it.In like manner, good works out of obedience to the law become mechanical and may bring only regret. Others have more fun, and it has often been said, "Everything fun is either immoral, illegal, or fattening." But good works flowing out of gratitude involve the response of love to life, others, and God. "... for the letter kills, but the Spirit gives life." The Spirit gives us freedom to use the law and not be used by it.

"Now the Lord is the Spirit, and where the Spirit of the Lord is, there is freedom." (2 Cor. 3:17) Growth in glory comes to us as we respond in freedom to the love of God. This is past the law. In this process Jesus is the example and the empowerer. He spoke on his own authority, not as the scribes, not as the legalists. We are summoned into a life like this. No law or Scripture phrase solves the problem for the Christian. Our own life must be brought into play. This is true in our relationship to a contemporary problem like homosexuality. How are we to relate to the homosexual? The easiest thing is to find some law, some statement, some prohibition, and by its use put the issue on the shelf. But the New Covenant, the new relationship, does not allow that. We are invited to respond in radical obedience to the love by which each one is loved. This does not give us the exact nature of the relationship; but it does push us to consider what love requires.

The Law can be read and agreed to. We can use it to judge others. Or, we can slavishly obey the law ourselves while wishing to disobey. The New Covenant, on the other hand, is life-giving and offers us a new heart. The Ten Commandments have their grandeur and glory and have meaning for today, but they need to be seen in the light of what has been revealed in the man Jesus. We have no bondage to a book. These Commandments can help us confront the Reality who loves us and who has revealed that love in creation, in history, and supremely in Jesus whom we call Christ. We are a people with a new look. "... for the letter kills, but the Spirit gives life."

2
AFFORDING LOVE

Commandments! Commandments! All our lives we have heard of commandments. We are commanded in the Hebrew Scriptures; we are commanded in the Christian texts. Not only does the Bible tell us what to do, our parents do or did as well. Our society tells us in the form of laws. Preachers tell us to do this, do that; be this, be that. No wonder commandments appear to us as a burden.

However, Jesus does more than impose laws upon us. He lifts humanity up into the presence of God and shows us our true nature. Ethical living is not so much laws as being what we are essentially and deeply. Jesus puts us in touch with our true humanity, living at its highest and best.

Holiness of Life

The issue is holiness of life. We don't especially like the word holy. Holy, we think, is being pious, sanctimonious, sober and serious. To be holy is to have no fun and to be headed for a narrowly defined religious life. The word is a much better one than we often think. Holiness is the nature of God. Holiness involves what is numinous and non-material. The holy leaves us feeling awe and wonder. What a mystery life is! The amazement that God is, that this world is, and that we are. We share in God's holiness, God's mystery.

To be holy is to be set apart as different. We are holy because we share in the nature of God. We are a reflection of God's glory. We are holy because God is holy. The attitude before holiness is reverence. Civilization rests on reverence. Without reverence we lose our humanity. To be without reverence is to be without soul. The holiness code in the Hebrew Scriptures and the Sermon on the Mount in Matthew have the loftiest moral and social commandments in all Scripture. In both Scriptures, we are directed away from revenge and retaliation, away from holding grudges, to loving the neighbor.

The Hebrews had brought from Babylonia, an eye for an eye ethic, the law of tit for tat. This is one of the earliest codes coming from Emperor Hammurabi about 2000 BCE. This law is repeated three times in Jewish Scripture. "If any harm follows, then you will give life for life, eye for eye, tooth for tooth, hand for hand, foot for foot, burn for burn, wound for wound, stripe for stripe." (Exodus 21:24) Is this savage and merciless? Not by any means. Tit for tat is the beginning of mercy and announces the limitation of vengeance. An eye for an eye is against the vendetta and blood feud in which all members of one group take the wrong out on all members of the other. Vengeance meant death, unlimited retaliation. Tit for tat limited retribution to the extent of the damage and became the means by which a judge assessed judgment.

Jesus took the whole matter a step further. Not only no vengeance, says Jesus, but no retaliation and no resentment. If someone strikes you on the right cheek, offer him the other. This is not primarily a word about violence. Think about another's right cheek. If you are right handed, how do you strike another? With the back of the hand! The right cheek meant an insult. If someone insults you, it does no good to respond in kind. The problem is theirs and not yours. Stand your ground.

If someone sues you for your coat, give him your cloak as well. The Jew had the legal right to the outer garment which served as both the covering and the blanket. The claimant could not keep that garment. Jesus is saying that his followers are not to pursue the legal claim to the limit and to be obsessed with legal rights. Moreover, if someone compels you to go one mile, go with him two. A member of the occupying forces of Rome had the right to call anyone into service to carry baggage. Jesus was saying that when you have to do something do it not only without resentment but with cheerfulness and grace. Think not of your liberty but of your duty and responsibility. (Matt. 5:38-42)

There are two ways of doing things. One is the irreducible minimum and nothing more. This indicates a hatred for the whole procedure. Or, do what you have to do and more—the something extra that renders a service to the other. Halford Luccock, in writing on this passage, refers to an eye-dropper religion that parcels out a drop of the self here and there, giving the absolute minimum and that's all.

Joy in life, holiness of life, is going beyond what is required. It is the difference between just mowing the lawn and also doing the trimming. It is the difference, as I remember from my childhood, of shoveling a narrow path through the snow or clearing the whole walk. Where is the satisfaction in life? Minimal living? Or, an expansive generosity of spirit that gives of oneself ungrudgingly and serves the other? Jesus points the way to satisfaction in life.

The Law of Love

Jesus departs from the old ethic in an even more radical way. Leviticus tells us: "... you are to love your neighbor as yourself." (Lev. 19:18) The neighbor for the ancient Hebrews was another Hebrew. They did not consider the enemy to be a neighbor. Jesus went further: "But I say to you, Love your enemies...." (Matt. 5:44) This expression of Christian love seems to be beyond us. But look at the kinds of love. "Storge" is family affection. "Philia" is a warm, relational love. "Eros" is the passion of sexual love. "Agape" is unconquerable benevolence and invincible good will.

Jesus never asked his followers to love enemies as they loved their dearest. Agape is an act of the will. It is the decision to be for those we don't like and who don't like us. Agape is seeking the highest good of the other. Loving the enemies is not liking them but wishing and willing for them fulness of life. Love is not Christian until it includes the love of the opposition, those who stand over against us.

How does this apply today? Though we cannot expect the Sermon on the Mount to be national policy; yet, for me, I cannot help but see nuclear arms in relationship to this text. Why do we have nuclear weapons? For a first strike capability at such time as we feel sufficiently threatened? The thought of our obliterating millions of people in such a strike is beyond my comprehension. In no way could this be love of the enemy. A first strike? Never!

We have nuclear arms to retaliate if the other side strikes first—so we hear. Think of that a moment. If we were the target of the first strike, thousands of us would be wiped out. Should we then retaliate? Vengeance would say yes. But to what end? The final chapter in civilization! That is the word from some in the scientific community. With two massive nuclear strikes the atmosphere of the northern hemisphere might be so contaminated as to destroy much of life. As it was said of old, I think it is still true: "'Vengeance is mine; I will repay, says the Lord.'" (Rom. 12:19)

The president of a university was asked his reaction to the discovery and release of nuclear power. He replied: "It is bad to know what God knows and not be like God."

The Expansiveness of Love

The Christian ethic involves love of the enemy. Why? What does it get us? I suspect that it would work better than what we are doing. Some evil is overcome with good. Not all to be sure! I am not an absolute pacifist. Some restraint, some power, is necessary to curb inhumanity. But the power of love has not been tried extensively.

Gandhi won his way by loving and revolutionized Indian society. Martin Luther King, Jr., with his non-violent approach to change, discovered a way to lead so many of his followers into a love that was in spite of: "We will match your capacity to inflict suffering with our capacity to endure suffering. We will meet your physical force with soul force. We will not hate you, but we cannot in all good conscience obey your unjust laws. Do to us what you will and we will still love you. Bomb our homes and threaten our children; send your hooded perpetrators of violence into our communities and drag us out on some side road, beating us and leaving us half dead, and we will still love you ... in winning our freedom we will so appeal to your heart and conscience that we will win you in the process."* Martin Luther King discovered that love filling the heart expels pride, anger, self-will and leads to rejoicing and a deep satisfaction.

But perhaps the best reason, the highest reason, for the Christian ethic of love is that it reflects the nature of God. It shares in the being of God. An old Rabbinic tale has angels singing after the Egyptian riders are lost in the sea. God is sorrowful. "The work of my hands is sunk in the sea, and you would sing before me. I take no pleasure in it."

In God is universal benevolence. We love in order to be the children of God—which is to say to be God-like, to be what we were intended. Both Scriptures agree. Love reflects the nature of our Creator. It is part of God's holiness. "You will be holy for I, am holy." (1 Peter 1:16) "Be perfect as your heavenly Father is perfect." (Matt. 5:48) He makes the sun rise on the evil and the good and rain to fall on the just and the unjust. God calls us to such a love.

The Christian ethic begins with God's love for us. We love because God first loved us. The love of God leads to the love of neighbor. It is the cement which holds life together. God's love knows no boundaries and includes the love of enemies. How do we know that God loves like that? How do I know? I have to trust and you have to trust. Trust me if you can. Trust Martin Luther, John Wesley, Francis Asbury, Thomas Acquinas, St. Augustine, Paul, Peter, and Jesus of Nazareth. We have innumerable witnesses.

We love because he first loved us. We are our true selves when we love others and do no harm even to our enemies. In the end will we make it? God gives us our freedom. Our love must be free and not forced. In Loren Eiseley's words ". . . For love is something that life in its prodigality could afford."** Evolution has come to this: either we find the will and the way to love or we will destroy ourselves. We can afford to love and take the risk because God has risked first. In the Jesus Christ

*Freely transcribed from a speech delivered at Western Michigan University on December 18, 1963.

***The Star Thrower*, Times Books, The New York Times Books Co., Inc., pg. 311.

event, is the demonstration that it is possible for us to love—even our enemies!

3
ON BEING MADE RIGHT

Life is filled with brokenness, separation, and suffering. We see these all about us, and we have experienced such in our own lives. We don't like this state and look for a way to guard against such experiences. No wonder that we are tempted to think of Christianity as preventive medicine.

How many identify Christianity with laws and rules to prevent brokenness. We think that doing right and not doing wrong will lead to a harmonious life free of much suffering. This is a heresy, a departure from the faith, a moralized Christianity made into a religion of rules and regulations complete with don'ts, mustn'ts, shouldn'ts, and can'ts. Such a view of Christianity puts chains around the faith and stifles its life.

The other side of the heresy sees that carefully doing the right thing earns the favor of God. As one unknown writer put it, "God gives us Heaven on the strengths of our moral report cards." This heresy says that God's love and grace have a price: good behavior. With our good behavior we try to justify ourselves before God. How easy it is to fall into this trap!

Our Standing in Life

How do we stand with God? Or, to put this another way: How do we stand with life? In one form or another each of us raises this question. Charlie Brown did once: *Lord, I have a question for you . Why am I sleeping in a cardboard box? Why do I have to suffer like this? Why me Lord? Don't answer that.* He was fearful that he was getting what he deserved, that he had no standing with God. We are suspicious that neither do we.

How *can* I be right? Let's face it. Many do not see this as a problem. God is, for them, a non-entity and is not involved.

This means that the self is the final arbiter and serves as God. The human, created to glorify God, chooses to glorify self and is corrupted in the process. Separation from fulness of life is the picture of our time. Not that we go around saying, "Woe is me. I am separated from God"; but our personal and social conflicts bear witness to the idolatry of self. Our guilt, our mental and spirutal disruption, bear testimony that we are not right.

Perhaps, though, that is not where many of us are. How do we stand with God? The hedonists among us may simply live as though whatever is behind it all doesn't care. Like our non-involved relationship with the teeming insect world in a forest, so God goes on God's way and we ours. Or, we may be Greeks, sensing the wrath of the gods. We are being pursued by the furies and being punished for all our wrongdoings, our false choices, and our selfishness.

How do we stand with God? The Hebrews found that they could not obey the law. Instead, they began the practice of the sacrifice. Everyone could manage a sacrificial offering to make things right with God. We are tempted to adopt this view. We can be made right by giving some big contribution to a cause, by spending our time doing good, by sacrificing our wants and needs to someone else's wants and needs. This is all commendable but fails to make us right.

Later the Hebrews returned again to the law with the Sadducces and Pharisees believing that the law could be kept. Obey the law and be right with God and all others. But the law has to be followed exactly. An extensive body of legal material was amassed to show people how to live by the law. This point of view has come through the centuries. Martin Luther felt the pressure: have I prayed enough? Such calculations drove him to despair. Some today are caught in this view of religion.

However, many of us may feel that we are not rigid legalists. Instead, we may try a modified version that proceeds like this: Perhaps we don't have to follow the law exactly. We are not perfect, and God understands our imperfections and accepts us on the basis of our trying. All we have to do is try. We make an effort to obey the Ten Commandments and the Golden Rule. And we do try and come closer than others we could mention.

In this way, we divide our world between those who strive to obey and those who don't; and we know on what side we place ourselves. We are made right, so we think, by trying. This is righteousness all right, self-righteousness!

Jesus knew that reliance on the law brings self-righteousness. He told the parable of the Pharisee and the Publican. "Two men went up to the temple to pray, one a Pharisee and the other a tax collector. The Pharisee, standing by himself, was praying thus, 'God, I thank You that I am not like other people: thieves, rogues, adulterers, or even like this tax collector. I fast twice a week; I give a tenth of all my income.' " (Luke 18:10-12) I heard of a pastor who preached on this text. As people were shaking his hand after the service, one person exclaimed, "That was a great sermon, pastor! I'm so glad I'm not like that old Pharisee!" That person missed the point. Jesus is saying that any attempt to consider ourselves right by comparison with others corrupts us. How, then, do we get right with God?

Getting Right

Paul lived for a time as a Pharisee, but he changed his perspective. He was converted from a Pharisee to a follower of Christ. He expressed himself forcefully by saying that all good deeds for the purpose of self-justification are so much rubbish. The word he used was excrement. All the doing that tries to make oursleves right is refuse. All our workaholism that is based on trying to prove that we are okay is worthless. (Phil. 3: 7-9) Paul gave up trying to create goodness on his own. He understood that we come to God in faith, not with accomplishments.

We suffer the loss of all things. We do our doing and then let go. We cannot hold on to our good deeds and expect to gain from them without becoming self-righteous. Doing brings us no merit. Not, "See! Look what I have done!" Do, by all means! Paul was a doer. But after the doing is done, give it up. Don't hold on to an expectation that it's going to justify you. All our doing is so much garbage, useless in terms of making us right.

The beginning of being right with God, with life, is giving

up our reliance on ourselves and our goodness. Even our best actions can have bad results. Our attempts to do good can have tragic consequences. Dr. Alice Cary, a medical missionary in Japan, reports of a case that illustrates this point. These are her words: "A man works as a janitor in a large school. He has a wife and four children with whom he cheerfully lives in two rooms, each ten feet square. Recently they received an urgent telegram from the wife's mother who, because of severe heart trouble, could no longer take care of herself. The janitor brought her to his tiny house, gave her half a room, and called a doctor. After listening to her heart and lungs, the doctor suspected far advanced tuberculosis rather than heart disease. An X-ray confirmed the suspicion: both lungs extensively diseased, a third of one lung gone. There was no hope for a cure. But It was essential that she be removed from her four grandchildren. It took three days of telephoning and searching to find a hospital bed for her.

"Meanwhile, the children stayed with neighbors. When the (elderly lady) was taken to the hospital, she turned against her daughter in rage, cursing her and accusing her of abandoning her to die. She refused to eat, and three days later she died alone, terrified, in wrath against her own family who were called but arrived too late.

"Could there be a more tragic death? And it was a needlessly tragic death, for if the doctor had not insisted on sending her away, she could have lived on somewhat happily as her grandchildren romped around her and her daughter waited on her. She would not have died feeling rejected, unloved, angry, and frightened. It is not pleasant for the doctor to think of that case. I know, for I am the doctor.

"Yet, it would have been wrong to let her stay on and let her infect those little children. To protect them was good, to condemn an old woman to die with hate, anger, and terror in her heart was certainly bad. I cannot forgive myself, even though I know that my intentions were good ethically speaking and my decision was right medically speaking. Still, I must bear the responsibility. Only God can forgive me, and I know that He has."

If a doctor, who in this particular case had no motive except healing and preventing misery, can cause such tragedy, how can we in our living believe that our well-intended acts are good and justify us? No, we cannot be self-righteous. Even our decisions may have tragic consequences. Faith in ourselves is not the answer.

Faith In the One

We are made right through faith, not in ourselves, but in God. Faith is the new creation where our boasting ends and we share in the righteousness of God. From one perspective the Christian way is not a religion at all. Paul Tillich in his writing tried to make this clear. All religions seem to reckon that human achievements constitute a claim on God and must be rewarded. Or, on the other hand, religions assume that human achievement is itself a reward of God proving the goodness of the one blessed. The Christian way, and it was first of all called "The Way," is to know the activity of God we call Christ.

Paul puts it well in Philippians: "I want to know Christ and the power of his resurrection...." (3:10) The dynamic movement in life is the movement from death to life. The resurrection story points to a bodily life that is worth living. This life involves brokenness, separation, and suffering. Nevertheless, this life can be raised up. The Christian way joins in the fellowship of his suffering. Jesus suffered defeat, loneliness, separation, pain. The message of the cross is that we cannot save ourselves. Jesus could not. He gave himself to God through a commitment to human need. Jesus could so concern himself about others, even at the moment of his suffering, because he had quit trying to save himself.

The Christian way is to be so united with him that we share in his death. We share where he walked; we experience his cross; we share his death. This means that we also can share the life that he continues to live. We can share his experiences. We do share the experiences of those whom we love and with whom we identify. We join with Christ along his way and become followers of the way.

Paul carries this another step: "... forgetting what lies behind and straining forward to what lies ahead...." This means never glorifying in our achievements or using them as an excuse for relaxing. The Christian forgets all he has done and looks ahead, without resting on his laurels. The way involves a forward movement. The image Paul uses is a foot race. With the mark ahead, we "press on toward the goal for the prize of the heavenly call of God in Christ Jesus." (Phil. 3:14) But to arrive at any mark is simply a moment to pause and get our breath before pressing on to the next one. Paul was not against doing. He was simply against doing to justify ourselves. The Christian life still takes discipline and effort and involves a reaching forward to what lies ahead.

We become right when we give up the rubbish of trying to justify ourselves by our doing and receive a relationship to God that makes us right. As His people we forget what is behind and press on in life and living. We can do this thanks to the confidence and trust that are the gifts of God that we see offered in the life of Jesus.

Bibliography

The Interpreter's Bible, Vol. 1, Abingdon-Cokesbury, N.Y. & Nashville, 1952.

Barclay, William, *The Ten Commandments for Today*, Harper & Row, New York, 1973.

Childs, Brevard S, *The Book of Exodus*, Westminster Press, 1974.

Clements, Ronald, *God's Chosen People*, SCM Press, 1968.

Hillers, Delbert R., *Covenant: The History of a Biblical Idea*, John Hopkins University Press, 1969.

Kalas, J. Ellswworth, *Ten Commandments From the Back Side*, Abingdon Press, Nashville, 1998.

Lehmann, Paul Lewis, *Decalogue and a Human Future*, W. B. Erdmans Co., 1995.

Neusner, Jacob, *How Judaism Reads the Torah*, P. Lang, N.Y. & Frankfurt, 1993.

Noth, Martin, *The Laws in the Pentateuch*, Fortress Press, Phil., 1967.

Shlain, Leonard, *The Alphabet Versus the Goddess*, Viking Penguin, 1998.

Stamm, J. J. & M.E. Andrew, *The Ten Commandments in Recent Research*, SCM Press, Ltd., London, 1967.

Timmerman, John H., *Do We Still Need the Ten Commandments?* Augsburg Press, Minn., 1997.

About the Author

GEORGE M. RICKER, Pastor Emeritus of University United Methodist Church in Austin, Texas, and has taught at Texas State University and Austin Presbyterian Theological Seminary. He presently serves as seminar director in the University of Texas SAGE (Seminars for Adult Growth and Enrichment) and QUEST continuing-education programs. He is the author of *What You Don't Have to Believe to be a Christian* (Eakin Press, 2002) and *The Faith Once Given* (Penpoint Press, 2004). He is also a lecturer, seminar leader, and newspaper columnist. His one-minute spots *Something to Think About* were featured on Austin radio some years ago.